Breakthrough

Praise for This Book

"This is not just a book for women. It's also for the men in our lives who care, value, and respect our contributions. Use this book as a conversation starter for those whose opinions you value and whose support you need. It's meant for dialogue. Conversations must happen between women at work, conversations with women friends in different fields, conversations with male coworkers, and conversations with friends. Finally, this book is meant to start a conversation with yourself. Don't push this book aside."

—Dr. Beverly Kaye, BevK&Co., coauthor, Love Em or Lose Em, Help Them Grow or Watch Them Go, Up Is Not the Only Way

*"For women, being well educated and competent is often **not** enough to achieve career success.*

In her book Breakthrough, *Saundra Stroope presents contemporary mythology versus reality, giving thoughtful insights into what gets us stuck. From our work in leadership and executive development, I'm convinced that knowing what to expect of ourselves and others can increase career success and satisfaction. This book is an excellent development tool for working women and the people who sustain them.*

It takes a lot longer to learn from experience than to tap into the wisdom Saundra Stroope condenses in her book. If you are embarking on a new career, getting promoted, changing careers, or staying put, reading this book will make life easier."

—Bonnie Hagemann, CEO, Executive Development Associates

Breakthrough

Career Strategies for Women's Success

Saundra Stroope

ılıBEP
BUSINESS EXPERT PRESS
Leader in applied, concise business books

Breakthrough: Career Strategies for Women's Success
Copyright © Business Expert Press, LLC, 2019.

First published in 2019 by
Business Expert Press, LLC
222 East 46th Street, New York, NY 10017
www.businessexpertpress.com

ISBN-13: 978-1-94897-628-2 (paperback)
ISBN-13: 978-1-94897-629-9 (e-book)

Business Expert Press Human Resource Management and Organizational Behavior Collection

Collection ISSN: 1946-5637 (print)
Collection ISSN: 1946-5645 (electronic)

Cover design by Charlene Kronstedt
Interior design by S4Carlisle Publishing Services Private Ltd., Chennai, India

First edition: 2019

10 9 8 7 6 5 4 3 2 1

Printed in the United States of America.

Dedication

To all the women and men who continuously support the advancement of women in the workplace

Abstract

It is an important time to celebrate the advancement of women. The number of women entrepreneurs, business owners, and leaders in corporate leadership roles is growing. However, there are still many challenges women face that are different from those of their male counterparts. Women sometimes have beliefs or career myths that may interfere with their personal career satisfaction and success.

The book is based on the input and advice gathered from of over 200 women across the globe. A survey of more than 180 women, interviews with over a dozen influential women in leadership and professional roles, and group meetings were conducted from January to March 2018. The women validated career myths that have an impact on their satisfaction at work and career success. The women also provided helpful tips, advice, and recommendations for helping women overcome challenges and achieve career success. This book explores the true barriers that women may encounter at work and offers you an opportunity to reflect on your strengths and development areas and create a plan for moving toward greater satisfaction and success in your career.

Key Words

women; career; career development; leadership; coaching; success; business; entrepreneurs; work satisfaction; professional development; gender differences

Contents

Acknowledgments

We can overcome our self-limiting beliefs, unintentional bias, and intentional discrimination only with ongoing encouragement, coaching, and guidance. Over 200 women across the globe participated in the creation of this book by offering their experiences, stories, and advice. Some women responded to an online survey, other women participated in interviews, and many shared stories during facilitated focus groups, educational sessions, and discussions with other women.

Thank you to all the women who participated in the survey, interviews, focus groups, and learning events. Special acknowledgment goes to Lynn Schmidt for collaborating and sharing her experience as an author. Her talent helped to create structure amid a multitude of stories and ideas. Kay Van Patter deserves praise for offering unfiltered opinions and edits during the book review process. Pamela Manson stepped in when needed to provide her editing and writing talent toward the completion of the book. The world would be a better place if all women and men behaved as these women and supported the career aspirations of women.

CHAPTER 1

Career Myths Impact Women's Success

The truth will set you free, but first it will piss you off.
—Gloria Steinem

It is an important time to celebrate the advancement of women. We have made visible progress in the last few decades. The number of women entrepreneurs, business owners, and leaders in corporate leadership roles is growing. However, there are still many challenges women face that are different than that from their male counterparts. Women sometimes have beliefs or career myths that may interfere with their personal career satisfaction and success.

A *myth* is defined in Dictionary.com as a traditional story, one concerning the early history of a people or social phenomenon. It's a widely held, but false, belief or idea. A myth is a misrepresentation of the truth. It might also be described as a folktale, legend, tall tale, or a cock-and-bull story. Women might choose to believe them for a variety of reasons. We want to believe that if we are committed, work hard, and assert ourselves, we will be recognized and rewarded. Managing our career and finding joy at work would be much simpler if our beliefs about work held true.

When we encounter a challenging situation at work that we aren't prepared to handle, it may be that the situation defies our preconceived beliefs about the way things should be in the work environment. It's important to reflect upon the ideas we have about work and identify those that are true and those that are myths. When the reality you are faced with at work doesn't align with your beliefs, you can overcome barriers by creating a clear plan to address the issues.

Over 200 women contributed their input about self-limiting false beliefs or career myths that had an impact on their satisfaction at work and career success. The women also provided helpful tips, advice, and recommendations for helping women overcome the challenges and achieve career success.

This book explores career myths and the true barriers that women may encounter at work. It offers you an opportunity to reflect on your strengths and development areas and create a plan for moving toward greater satisfaction and success in your career. Your commitment to your own development and to helping women advance is appreciated.

The Top Five Career Myths

While every woman's story is unique, not every woman will experience every myth in her career. These five career myths were the most commonly selected on the global survey and in group meetings as having a detrimental impact on women's career success. Women from the ages of 18 to 53 responded to the survey. Approximately 80 percent of the respondents were from the United States. Women from Europe, Canada, Australia, New Zealand, Asia, South America, and Africa participated in the survey.

1. **Women can expect to be compensated fairly and rewarded for their contributions in the workplace.** While negotiation skills can be learned, this issue is much more complex than mastering the art of the "ask" alone. This means understanding the unique value that your talent brings to an organization, and how your work contributes to achieving business goals.

2. **Women's skills and experience matter more than their communication style and appearance.** Women are often judged as less competent based upon their physical appearance alone. Focusing your development plan on the skills and knowledge that is needed to advance in your current role or obtain your next position may not be enough to overcome this bias.

3. **If women are assertive and drive for results, it will always benefit their career.** Women who demonstrate strength and assertiveness may be judged negatively. Women must carefully strike a balance

between the focus on results and relationships to move forward in a career. We haven't yet overcome the social expectation that women are the primary caregivers in the family and that a successful career may be viewed as a distraction.

4. **Advancement for women is dependent only on performing well.** There are many reasons that women may not advance even when they have the knowledge, skills, and experience to perform a job. Women need to be aware, informed, and coached to overcome barriers. Leaders need to ensure that workload distribution and performance measures are consistently fair across all team members.

5. **Men and women believe in equality for women.** While many men and women support the advancement of women in the workplace, both men and women have unconscious biases. We are all guilty. This calls for all of us to increase our own self-awareness. We can only overcome unintentional discriminatory behaviors when we know of them and take action.

How to Use This Book

- Read, reflect, and assess your own satisfaction and success.
- Create a development plan to leverage your strengths and grow in opportunity areas.
- Ask for feedback and input from trusted friends, colleagues, managers, mentors, and coaches.
- Find other women and men who will support your career development.
- Share your development plan with them.
- Revisit and update your development plan on an ongoing basis.

CHAPTER 2

Myth: Women's Skills and Experience Matter More Than Communication Style and Appearance

Never bend your head. Always hold it high. Look the world straight in the eye.

—Helen Keller

A news anchor for an Australian TV morning show wore the same blue suit day in and day out for over a year. Aside from occasional dry cleaning, there were no wardrobe, accessory, or hairstyle changes. In this age of social media commentary, no one noticed the suit or provided remarks on anything but the news stories covered. They paid attention only to the skillful level of coverage provided that year. He was male.

This story reported by the Sydney Morning Herald didn't hold true for his colleague, a female newscaster named Lisa Wilkinson. Once in the public eye, Wilkinson quickly discovered that her choice of clothing, accessories, and hairstyle sometimes generated a bigger reaction from male and female viewers than the actual news story she was covering regardless of how important or political the issue was. She received countless e-mails and letters from audience members containing unsolicited fashion advice, urging her to "get some style." One well-meaning fan went as far as to send her a letter suggesting she choose colors in her wardrobe that do not clash with the couch.

It is the reality for many women. A search by name on the Internet about any woman from a globally known presidential candidate, a prime minister, or CEO to a locally known attorney or school principal will reveal opinions about her dress and mannerisms that may be deemed by critics as unstylish, distracting, or inappropriate for the role. Hillary Clinton's choice of pantsuit is mocked routinely on Saturday Night Live in the United States. In the United Kingdom, Theresa May caused a Twitter firestorm by showing cleavage during a budget announcement in the House of Commons. During the controversial Nicole Brown Simpson and Ron Goldman murder trial, deemed the legal trial of the century, attorney Marcia Clark's change of hairstyle was news. A study by Pew Research confirms that Americans rate physical attractiveness as the most valuable trait for women followed by empathy, nurturing, and kindness. They found that honesty and morality are the most valuable traits for men followed by professional and financial success.

While fashion in itself may be an interesting topic, it has little to do with the amount of talent, skill, or experience a woman has. It has even less to do with performance outcomes in her job. It's hard to find this type of attention and criticism based on appearance for a male performing a similar role. Appearance is considered to be part of the business equation for men and women when it comes to good hygiene and blatant disrespect for established dress codes. In the mid-1970s and 1980s, the term "dress for success" became popular after the publication of books on the topic. In the books by John Molloy, he noted the special challenge for women to try to fit in and to look like a traditionally white male workforce. Men only need to worry about professional attire, while women also need to worry about their gender in the workplace. Since then, many organizations have adopted casual dress codes, which can make the wealth of fashion choices available even more perplexing for women when it comes to managing impressions.

There are some physical characteristics like height, body style, sex, and attractiveness that can't be changed easily. Research in the *Journal of Applied Psychology* confirms a correlation between physical qualities like our height and potential income. Taller individuals are perceived by others as more influential and report higher earnings than individuals with comparable skills and experience. Assumptions about your position, responsibilities, and skills may be made by others based on your physical appearance alone. For example, when you walk into a room with a taller person, people may assume the other person has more power, status, or influence.

A study in the *Journal of Humanities and Social Science* also confirms there are differences in the way that women and men communicate. Most women are socialized at a young age to behave in a manner that is more amiable, people-oriented, and nurturing than men. A woman's communication style has the goal of building relationships with others. A woman will usually downplay her accomplishments and communicate more indirectly. She will spend time building rapport and take turns when talking with others. When it comes to nonverbal communication, a woman will smile more often than a man and use a variety of facial expressions during a conversation.

Most men, on the other hand, are socialized from a very young age to achieve and accomplish tasks. When they communicate, they express status, report on their accomplishments, give advice, and solve problems. A man's communication style has the goal of demonstrating knowledge about the topic. He will express his opinion bluntly and spend little time discussing personal topics. A man's social banter will focus on facts such as the score of a recent sporting event. A man will show less emotion, listen selectively, and make less eye contact during a conversation.

In the workplace, when women communicate directly in a nonstereotypical manner they can be met with harsh criticism. Labels like bossy, pushy, threatening, controlling are used to describe a woman who uses the same type of direct, task-oriented communication most often used by men at work. Communicating more indirectly certainly isn't the answer. It's a bit of a catch-22 for women. A woman is often viewed as too soft, indecisive, or incompetent if she communicates in a stereotypically feminine way. Communicating in a direct and self-confident manner is important.

Women who use a more subtle stereotypically feminine approach may have important ideas overlooked. Using words like "just" and "sorry" signals uncertainty to others. Asking permission to speak or making suggestions with a questioning tone of voice also undermine your own competence. Here is an example of how this may play out at work.

A group has gathered to work on an important business challenge. The goal of the meeting is to brainstorm approaches and agree to the best course of action. Several men dominate the conversation. They interrupt each other with new ideas, often appearing as though they want to prove their idea is better than the last.

A woman sits quietly in a chair along the side of the room. She listens attentively to each new idea that is presented. She makes a few notes on a notepad. Suddenly, she realizes the overriding themes in the data and has a breakthrough solution. Rather than interrupting, she waits patiently until the end of the meeting. Then she asks, "May I offer an idea?" She states the solution, and the problem is solved once and for all. The team is ecstatic and agrees quickly.

As the team members exit the room, several of them thank the male team member who has been sitting at the head of the table for setting up the meeting and his leadership in solving business issue. This issue might not have been solved if she had not been in the room. Her feminine approach may make her appear less competent or less deserving of praise for her contribution. This woman may actually be the leader on this team, driving the group toward consensus.

It is clear that women are frequently viewed as less competent, less experienced, and as having less impact on the work they are performing based on their appearance and communication style. Without understanding this reality, women may dedicate their professional development time to learning new skills and gaining experience. Then they are shocked to learn that there are subtleties in their appearance and communication style, which are just as important when it's time to receive a job offer, promotion, or new title at work.

Success Strategies

There are two key strategies for overcoming this myth. First, develop a personal presence, and then balance your communication style.

Develop a Personal Presence

Know your brand. Think about your appearance and nonverbal communication and decide how you want others to view you. This means being your authentic self and knowing that in the world we live in, whether you like it or not, people will make judgments about you based on the way you look. Your personal presence will have an impact on your career.

Your physical appearance, dress, and nonverbal communication have an impact on the perceptions of others. Think about this carefully and consider the personal brand or image you want to have. Ask yourself, "What is the first thought you want people to have when they see me?" Then consider personal attributes that you want to change to create a positive impression.

Dress the part. Like an actress dresses the part of a role for a movie, consider the role you perform at work now or the one you want to perform in the future and dress for the part. Although many corporations have relaxed dress codes, there are always unwritten social norms that guide the way we dress depending on the company culture. Even the Royal Family has guidelines on how they will dress for public occasions.

The Queen of England often dresses in bright colors because she wants to be seen in a large crowd. If your role doesn't call for you to be the visible center of attention, you may want to reconsider vivid colors, wild patterns, cold shoulders tops, large ruffles, nail art, tattoos, ear gauges, nose rings, bold accessories, or fashion trends that may distract attention from the message you want to send others when you walk into a room. Your appearance reflects how you feel about yourself, your role, and your company.

Balance Your Communication Style

The communication goals most commonly sought by women and men, building relationships and demonstrating knowledge, are equally good. The best communicators learn to strike an effective balance between building solid connections with people and driving results. They can influence others, show empathy, express information, and solve complex business problems with innovative solutions.

Find a role model. Find examples of successful, well-respected female and male communicators within your organization. Watch their behavior and observe the way they state their message and include others in two-way dialogue. People adapt their communication approaches every day depending on the audience and the situation. Consider the culture of the company where you work and the needs of the people you interact with in your role.

Ask for input. Talk to people and ask for input on your personal communication strengths. Listen carefully to their suggestions. Consider feedback you have received in the past about times when you were perceived as too pushy, and times you should have spoken up. Then, set intentional goals for improving your communication. Don't be afraid to change your approach, but be authentic and make changes that will work for you. There isn't one perfect way to communicate in every situation.

Flex your communication style to fit the situation. In situations where you have been told that your approach is too forceful, think about defining the situation and making subtle, meaningful adjustments in the way you deliver the message. You might focus on changing your facial expression, emotion, or tone while delivering the same type of information. There is a fine line between letting people know about your accomplishments and bragging. The words you use to frame your point are important. Think about what you want to say and how you will say it before voicing your opinion, especially when emotions are strong.

Engage others to gain their support and build relationships. Many times asking for input will engage people with strong egos, personalities, or opinions in the solution. It may be helpful to meet with key stakeholders who will be attending a meeting prior to the event as part of your preparation. Ask questions and gather information even if you think you already know the answer. You may receive a different response from others with small changes in your approach.

If you receive feedback that you need to appear more self-confident with others, think about how you will contribute your ideas. At times during meetings, you may need to repeat your point. Sometimes others try to take over or hijack an idea that you present. Interject at the moment and politely thank them for their support. You must be prepared to maintain control and claim your ideas with confidence to influence others. Don't wait for others to offer opportunities or ask for your input on important projects. Take the initiative to volunteer to lead a new project or offer your input.

Small behaviors like sitting in a chair along the side of the room during a meeting rather than sitting at the conference table can have a big impact on the perception of your intended contribution. Research by Dr. Albert Mehrabian shows that the words we use when we communicate to others account for only 7 percent of what is communicated. Other subtle cues derived from our appearance, body language, gestures, vocal tone, and posture communicate volumes about us and the message we send to others.

When you accomplish significant results, don't wait for others to notice. Communicate clearly with your manager, colleagues, and subordinates about the actions you took and the impact it made on the business. One easy method for bringing your results to the attention of others is by sending an e-mail or presenting a brief overview of the outcomes at the end of a project.

If your manager gives you the opportunity to provide written input on your formal performance evaluation, be very clear about your successes. Some women unintentionally sabotage themselves by sharing too much of their own self-criticism. Imagine as though you are writing the report to help your manager justify a raise, special bonus, new position, or promotion for you. Find ways to quantify your results and identify the benefits your performance had for the company. Focus on your strengths, what you accomplished, and the impact it made for the customer. Talk about how you will leverage your strengths. The criticism you have for yourself can be used to improve your performance next time.

When you have differences of opinion, there are a variety of approaches to communicating with others. Not every conflict needs to be addressed, but you want to be sure that you aren't avoiding the hard conversations that need to happen. If an issue is unimportant or has little impact on results, it may not be worth addressing. Relying on any one approach like consensus building, accommodating, or competing can reduce your effectiveness. Learn to read the situation and adapt the way you approach differences intentionally.

Practice. Practicing new communication approaches at every opportunity is important, even if the new method is uncomfortable at first. It often helps to practice with a trusted colleague or a small group of people before presenting to a key customer, executive leadership, or larger audience. Confidence in your ability to communicate effectively improves with experience.

Your skills and experience deserve recognition. Balanced communication is the key to allowing others to discover them. Remain true to yourself. Find your authentic personal presence and your unique voice and your talent will be evident.

Assess Yourself and Plan for Development

This purpose of self-assessment is to help you enhance your effectiveness. This tool can help you chart your progress over time. It can also help you discover your strengths and development areas. Use the information to guide discussions with your manager and others in your network who can support your career development. You may also use the questions to solicit feedback from others.

Assess Yourself

Instructions: Read each question item and rate yourself on a scale of 1 to 5.

- 1 = I need serious improvement in this area.
- 2 = I need some improvement in this area.
- 3 = I'm talented and skilled in this area.
- 4 = A strength for me.
- 5 = A major strength. I consider myself a role model for other women.

Chapter 2 Assessment Questions	Rating				
1. I am aware of the way I am perceived by others in my appearance, body language, and nonverbal communication.	1	2	3	4	5
2. I have a personal brand or image that will have a positive impact on my career.	1	2	3	4	5
3. I dress appropriately for the role I play in the organization.	1	2	3	4	5
4. I observe others who communicate effectively for cues about the best way to communicate within the culture.	1	2	3	4	5
5. I gather input from others on my communication strengths and development areas.	1	2	3	4	5
6. I can adapt my communication style to fit the situation.	1	2	3	4	5
7. I can reduce my assertiveness when needed with changes in my facial expression, emotion, or tone.	1	2	3	4	5
8. I engage with others to build relationships and support for my ideas when needed.	1	2	3	4	5
9. I can communicate with increased confidence when needed, maintain control, and claim my ideas to influence others.	1	2	3	4	5
10. I try new communication approaches when given the opportunity.	1	2	3	4	5
Calculate Your Overall Average Rating					

Plan for Development

Reflect on your assessment score and plan for your future. If your overall average rating is a 4 or 5, personal presence and communication style is a strength for you. If your average rating is a 1, 2, or 3, presence and communication style could become a career derailer. On the question items where you rated yourself a 4 or 5, consider new ways to leverage your strengths. If you rated yourself a 1, 2, or 3, consider the implications for your career. These areas could get in the way of your future success. Use the ideas for leveraging strengths and developing opportunity areas to create a plan for career development.

Leverage strengths

- Continue to build your personal brand and adapt your style to the audience (senior executives, employees, customers).
- Think of new ways to communicate with others and continue to practice new communication methods.

- Mentor or coach another woman on ways to adapt her communication style to become more effective at influencing others.
- Speak to a group of women about the importance of presence and communication.

Develop opportunities
- Clarify what is most important to you and define actions you can take to improve your presence and communication style.
- Tailor your appearance, presence, and communication style to fit the situation.
- Talk with your manager and others about their perceptions of you and clarify where you can be more effective in your communication with others.
- Identify new communication approaches you will take and practice using them with others.

Additional Resources

Booher, D. November, 2011. Communicate with Confidence: How to Say It Right the First Time and Every Time. New York, NY: McGraw-Hill Education.

Booher, D. October, 2011. Creating Personal Presence: Look, Talk and Act Like a Leader. Oakland, CA: Berrett-Koehler Publishers.

The Myers-Briggs Company. "The TKI Conflict Mode Assessment." https://www.themyersbriggs.com/en-US/Products-and-Services/TKI

CPP, Inc. March, 2014. "Four Tips for Managing Conflict," *YouTube*. https://www.youtube.com/watch?v=QJiJ95mHftE

Cuddy, A. June, 2012. "Your Body Language May Change Who You Are," *Ted Talks*. https://www.ted.com/talks/amy_cuddy_your_body_language_shapes_who_you_are

Cuddy, A. January, 2018. *Presence: Bringing Your Boldest Self to Your Biggest Challenges*. London, England: The Orion Publishing Group Ltd.

DefMethod. 2017. "Just Not Sorry, The Gmail Plug-In," *Chrome Web Store*. https://chrome.google.com/webstore/detail/just-not-sorry-the-gmail/fmegmibednnlgojepmidhlhpjbppmlci

CHAPTER 3

Myth: If Women Are Assertive and Drive for Results, It Will Always Benefit Their Careers

My mother told me to be a lady.
And for her, that meant to be your own person, be independent.

—Ruth Bader Ginsburg

Confidence, assertiveness, strength, bravery, independence, courage, intelligence, and success; these are the traits admired in a businessman, and sometimes in a woman. At times they are not. An outgoing, well-educated, professional woman named Heidi Roizen spent a decade networking, leading others, and building a successful software company. When researchers at Columbia University changed her name to Howard in the Harvard Business Review Case and asked some students to evaluate Heidi and others to look at Howard, the results were astonishing. The good news is that both Heidi and Howard were found to be equally competent. The bad news is that the students who participated in the study evaluated Heidi as less worthy of a promotion, more self-serving, and less likable.

Perhaps this issue hasn't changed much for women since the 1800s. In that era, Annie Oakley rose to the height of fame as a sharpshooter in Buffalo Bill's Wild West Show. Oakley was respected for her talent as an outstanding shot and her ladylike behavior. She was nicknamed "America's Sweetheart" and the "Princess of the West." She toured the globe, met with the Queen of England, and won numerous awards.

Oakley was enthusiastic about sharing her talent and skills for the good of her country. She offered to train and form an army of women sharpshooters for two U.S. presidents. Her letters were simply ignored. She was also attacked by newspaper publisher William Randolph Hearst, who ran a false story alleging theft and cocaine abuse. It took 7 years of her life and she lost thousands of dollars defending her reputation in 55 lawsuits against the newspapers. This was certainly a devastating personal experience and significant expense.

We are no longer held to the Victorian standards for what it means to be a lady. Even today, the definition of career women in the *MacMillan Dictionary* defines "career woman" as something many people view as a bad thing. In an article for *Psychology Today*, one psychologist proposed that there are many reasons people don't like smart women. One of the most apparent is the idea that smart women don't make good servants. We have not yet overcome the social expectation that women are the primary caregivers in the family and that a successful career may be a distraction.

Moving forward in a career requires walking a tightrope. It's as though you are walking across a tiny line, wobbling back and forth, making constant small adjustments to your position while always at the risk of a dangerous fall to the ground. You must take ownership of your career and display assertiveness to advance. This behavior must be perfectly balanced somewhere between being completely passive and on the other side being overly aggressive. This also means striking the perfect balance between building relationships with others and driving for results as you manage your career.

Researchers at Proctor and Gamble in the Philippines found that 70 percent of men and 58 percent of women agreed that women are required to downplay their personalities to be accepted by others. With this information, they launched an award-winning advertising campaign. In one of the ads, the images of a man and woman appear demonstrating similar behavior like speaking in front of an audience. The man's behavior is labeled with positive words like persuasive, dedicated, or smooth. The woman's behavior is branded with negative words like pushy, selfish, or show-off. It may work well for men to proclaim their career goals loudly and share their accomplishments. Muhammad Ali was well known for telling everyone "I am the greatest" of all time or "I am the best." He even once said "I am not the greatest. I am the double greatest." It is not uncommon for a man to share with everyone at the office that he is interested in sitting in the corner office one day or wants to be promoted to a higher level position. Sometimes men declare themselves as the future leader, even as they are just entering a company in an entry level role. This same approach to sharing future career aspirations is unlikely to be effective for women.

Marcia Reynolds wrote in *The Huffington Post* that it is vital that women learn to manage relationships across the organization that you work in, with your manager, and outside of your organization. It clearly isn't enough to focus only on developing work-related skills and driving for results. In a documentary titled *RBG*, about the life of U.S. Supreme Court Justice Ruth Bader Ginsburg, the filmmakers give a lot of credit to her husband, Marty Ginsburg, for supporting her career. At a critical moment when a position became available, it was Marty who began lobbying throughout Washington D.C. for her advancement.

Justice Ginsburg was clearly determined to succeed in her profession and had a noteworthy record of accomplishments at that time. Her relationship with her husband and others in her profession also had a profound impact on her success. Many of the people interviewed in the film talk about her quiet, demure, or introverted nature. She has become well known for her dissenting opinions. When she speaks, she offers her different perspective very slowly and deliberately. Assertiveness and ladylike behavior can coexist. It means having the confidence to express your opinions, while respecting others.

Many women struggle to find the right level of assertiveness. A study of career management techniques by Springer Science and Business Media confirmed that there are negative repercussions for women who display behaviors more commonly used by men like self-promotion, competing with others, or claiming responsibility for success. The challenge for women is that if we display only more traditionally feminine, passive, and modest behavior, we may be overlooked when it comes time to reward performance, offer promotions, or assign opportunities for development.

Researchers at Tilburg University found that, in fact, women do have fewer challenging experiences on the job when compared to men. In their study, senior-level managers were more likely to give the assignments to men. The opportunity to learn from experience and gain new skills is critical to career development. For this reason, many women choose to leave corporate work environments. They decide to start their own businesses and become entrepreneurs.

Felena Hansen is an entrepreneur and the Founder of Hera Hub, a collaborative and shared office workspace for women. Hansen wrote an article for *Entrepreneur Magazine* stating that the reason many women start their own businesses is that they want to make a meaningful difference, and their opinions are not valued in traditional corporate work environments. Entrepreneurship is certainly an option, but brings its own set of dynamics that may not eliminate the assertiveness tightrope issue for women.

Empowered women business owners must interact with clients, suppliers, and competitors. The same perceptions about assertive behavior may have an impact on their success as they work toward building a company, communicating a vision, and obtaining resources or financing from others.

An ancient Greek philosopher named Heraclitus said, "Dogs bark at what they don't understand." When women violate the role expectations of stereotypically feminine behavior ingrained in society, many people still find it hard to comprehend. You may be criticized harshly for having the guts to move your career forward assertively. It may even harm your career by having a negative impact on your position or income. It's important to acknowledge that women who demonstrate strength and assertiveness are often judged negatively. When you are aware of these perceptions and the potential impact, you can take positive action to prevent them from sabotaging your future success.

Success Strategies

There are three strategies for overcoming this myth, demonstrate self-confidence, build relationships, and find the right fit for your style.

Demonstrate Self-Confidence

Manage your emotions. There will undoubtedly be times in your career that you will be on the receiving end of unwarranted negative criticism.

The key to remaining self-confident and assured is being able to manage emotions of anger, self-doubt, or fear at these times. Any time you receive feedback, it's important to remain calm and listen carefully for any information that may be helpful. There may be facts that you haven't considered or small adjustments you can make to your approach that will make a huge difference in your results. You must have the confidence to believe in yourself and know that you deserve to achieve success.

Remember that responding to any form of negativity in anger will not help you move toward your goals. Sometimes restating the message that you have received before you respond will help the other person feel you have heard. Then you can respond to the message in a confident manner, indicating the action you will take, if any, in response to the data shared. A simple statement letting the other person know that you disagree with him or her may be enough to show that you are confident in your position.

Think it through. In other words, pick your battles carefully. If an issue is important to you and the organization, it may be important to assert yourself strongly in the situation. Even then, assess your audience. Think about how others in the organization may respond and if they will resist or support your position. Then evaluate their readiness to support you, the risk of speaking up, and plan your approach to give yourself the highest chance of success. There may be times when the risk of asserting yourself is too high. In a politically charged, uncertain situation, you may decide to remain silent for a while or gather more information. There is no harm in using the good qualities associated with being feminine or ladylike in any situation. It usually means showing empathy, being cour-teous to others, and listening well.

If you receive specific feedback that you are too assertive and need to soften your approach, one way to handle this is to think through the full situation. Think about the key people involved, the departments, the group of coworkers, or customers and their preferences. Ask yourself, "If I were a man, would I have received this input?" If the answer is yes, then consider taking a different approach. If the answer is no, you may want to have a more in-depth conversation with the person to explain your concerns. Most of the time the best approach toward a respectful, productive solution is talking directly with the person first, rather than immediately involving a third party or launching a formal complaint to others not involved.

Manage Stress. Remaining confident in the face of opposition requires that you may need to develop thick skin in some situations. This means listening, but not letting the other person's message cause undue stress for you internally. Caring for yourself in stressful situations is important. It may be helpful to disengage from the conversation at times and return to it at a mutually agreed upon date and time. Even a small break, like taking a walk outside the office with a breeze of fresh air and trees surrounding you may give you the confidence boost you need. Focus on what the other person needs from you and what you need from him or her to reach your goal rather than taking any criticism personally.

Stay focused on your career. You know your own experience, personality, and talents better than anyone else. Be true to yourself and stay focused on your career goals despite the barriers that arise. Career ownership means creating a vision for your career, taking the responsibility for decisions, and setting your direction. You are the one who ultimately will decide how to respond to any setbacks and determine the next step you will take in your career. Accept that in life, you are responsible for your success and others won't always appreciate or thank you for the work you do. You must be authentic, define what success means to you, and feel that your work is meaningful. Above all else, stay focused, keep your hand on the wheel, and keep driving forward.

Build Relationships

Find trusted supporters. It is important to have a diverse group of other people in your career network that you trust. When you face career challenges, you will need the support of others to help you overcome the barriers. There are a wealth of women's organizations dedicated to the empowerment of women. There are also many men that can be trusted to support your career goals. Having a diverse group of trusted supporters and mentors that includes women and men within and outside the organization will be most helpful to you.

Women have shared concerns on social media and the Internet understandably about the concepts of "mansplaining" and "hepeat," where a man gets credit for your idea by repeating it. In many organizations, the majority of people in powerful positions are still men. It may be helpful to enlist the support of a man you trust to restate your position while giving the appropriate recognition to you. It's a matter of finding other key influencers, whether they are women or men, to support your position. If the senior-level positions in the company are held by men and you want to increase your visibility, it helps to have the support of men in that group.

Balance results and relationships. Walking the assertiveness tightrope requires that you constantly make adjustments to your approach. Monitor others reactions while you drive for producing quality results and maintaining positive relationships. Manage assertiveness carefully and understand the difference between being assertive and aggressive. Dictionary.com defines aggressive behavior as hostile, belligerent, antagonistic, and ready to attack. Most people have experienced working with overly aggressive men and women in their careers, few seem to enjoy it. You are striving to be confident, self-assured, and decisive; not aggressive.

Communicate strategically. Make sure that others know that you have the goals of the organization in mind when you move forward assertively. Finding a common strategic goal will help you build relationships across departmental boundaries where there may be competition for resources. Communicate about how your goals support the overall business strategy or the customer. Asking others to support your initiative may be perceived as too pushy or self-serving if you haven't communicated the business reason or the benefits to the organization.

Find the right fit. The best time to assess the company culture is when you are interviewing for a new role. It's important to look at more than just the job description and whether or not you have the ability to perform the work. Assess the big picture by asking about the company culture and values. Pay attention to the way you and others are treated during the interview process. Look for subtle cues as to how you will be treated as a team member.

Surround yourself with people who you will enjoy. Look for people who respect you, your experience, your opinions, your strengths, and the talent you will bring to the organization. The right fit for you may mean starting your own business, rather than a corporate environment.

Assess Yourself and Plan for Development

This purpose of self-assessment is to help you enhance your effectiveness. This tool can help you chart your progress over time. It can also help you discover your strengths and development areas. Use the information to guide discussions with your manager and others in your network who can support your career development. You may also use the questions to solicit feedback from others.

Assess Yourself

Instructions: Read each question item and rate yourself on a scale of 1 to 5.

- 1 = I need serious improvement in this area.
- 2 = I need some improvement in this area.
- 3 = I'm talented and skilled in this area.
- 4 = A strength for me.
- 5 = A major strength. I consider myself a role model for other women.

Chapter 3 Assessment Questions	Rating				
1. I can remain self-confident and assured when I receive negative feedback from others.	1	2	3	4	5
2. I am aware of my emotions and I can listen and respond to others without anger or self-doubt.	1	2	3	4	5
3. I think through the situation and assert myself on important and meaningful issues.	1	2	3	4	5
4. I can manage stress and disengage from a conflict temporarily if I need time to consider my response.	1	2	3	4	5
5. I accept responsibility for my career success, stay true to my goals, and find ways to overcome barriers.	1	2	3	4	5
6. I can build relationships with a diverse network of people, women and men, who will support my career.	1	2	3	4	5
7. I can balance my attention on achieving results and building solid relationships with others.	1	2	3	4	5
8. I act with decisive assertiveness that is not viewed as aggression.	1	2	3	4	5
9. I can communicate strategically when asserting my views and can explain the business reasons for my opinions.	1	2	3	4	5
10. I consider the organizational fit in addition to my skills when making career decisions.	1	2	3	4	5
Calculate Your Overall Average Rating					

Plan for Development

Reflect on your assessment score and plan for your future. If your overall average rating is a 4 or 5, personal presence and communication style is a strength for you. If your average rating is a 1, 2, or 3, presence and communication style could become a career derailer. On the question items where you rated yourself a 4 or 5, consider new ways to leverage your strengths. If you rated yourself a 1, 2, or 3, consider the implications for your career. These areas could get in the way of your future success. Use the ideas for leveraging strengths and developing opportunity areas to create a plan for career development.

Leverage strengths

- Reflect on your career and identify one or two past challenges that at the time seemed insurmountable. Write down the specific actions you took to overcome the issue you faced. Keep these actions in mind the next time you face a challenge.
- Talk with other women about the techniques you have used to remain self-confident and assertive in the face of career opposition.
- Continue to build relationships by setting a goal to reach out to one or two new departments or professional networks related to your profession or career path.
- Introduce other women to people in your network who support assertiveness and career development for women.

Develop opportunities

- Make a conscious effort to listen carefully before responding to input from others.
- Communicate strategically with others, emphasizing the overall business case or the benefits for organization, when asserting your viewpoint.
- Talk with people you trust about their perceptions of your assertiveness, and ask for different ways to approach situations in which you might be viewed as overly aggressive.
- Create a vision for your career that includes both the type of work you want to perform and the type of work environment that needs to be present in the organization.

- Weigh the risks associated with speaking up in your organization. Ask yourself, "What is the worst thing that could happen, if I speak up in this situation?" Make sure the issue is truly important when you demonstrate assertiveness.

Additional Resources

Bradberry, T., and J. Greaves. June, 2009. *Emotional Intelligence 2.0.* San Diego, CA: TalentSmart; Har/Dol En edition.

Carnegie, D. October, 1988. *How to Win Friends and Influence People.* New York, NY: Simon & Schuster.

Dweck, C. S. December, 2007. *Mindset: The New Psychology of Success.* New York, NY: Ballantine Books.

Ferrazzi, K. June, 2014. *Never Eat Alone: And Other Secrets to Success One Relationship at a Time.* New York, NY: Penguin Random House LLC.

Kaye, B. September, 2017. *Up Is Not the Only Way; Rethinking Career Mobility.* Seattle, WA: Fierce, Inc.

Murphy, J. November, 2011. *How to Stand Up for Yourself Assertiveness and Still Win the Respect of Others.* Scotts Valley, CA: Createspace Independent Pub.

Patterson, K., and J. Grenny. September, 2011. *Crucial Conversations Tools for Talking When the Stakes are High.* New York, NY: McGraw Hill Education.

Phelps, S., and N. Austin. June, 2002. *The Assertive Woman.* Los Angeles, CA: Impact Publishers.

CHAPTER 4

Myth: Advancement for Women Is Only Dependent on Performing Well

I never realized until lately that women are supposed to be the inferior sex.

—Katherine Hepburn

She is on top of the world. The CEO of her company is meeting with her in person to offer congratulations, hand her the award certificate and reward check. Her innovative idea and her leadership guiding the new program from conception to implementation have garnered praise from coworkers, suppliers, and customers. She achieved the impossible. During a time of significant business challenge, she led the team to new levels of production and higher quality results.

Six months later, her male colleague is promoted to the role of manager, overseeing her department. He will represent the department and her work in future meetings with corporate executives and community governance committees composed of key customers. She contemplates what it will be like to report to a person who has been with the company only a few short months. She wonders if her management really understood her loyalty to the company, the difficulties she had to overcome in leading the recent project to success, and her record of past accomplishments. She dreams of leading the department one day and is puzzled about her future career path. She also realizes that her current role is pretty good. Not many others in the organization receive the attention and recognition she is given. People praise her work, she has good pay, and she is able to spend time with her family.

We don't know the next step she will take in her career. We do know that ultimately it is up to her to decide whether to stay at her current level or advance. It is also up to her to define her unique vision of career success. People thought of career success for many years as reaching the next rung in the career ladder. In today's business environment with the growth of the freelance economy, many people are defining success more holistically. Perhaps success means earning a good wage and enjoying time away from work. She may have the desire, drive, ambition, and competitive spirit to advance. She may decide to avoid the risk of leaving a nice, well-paying job.

There are many reasons that women may not advance, even when they have the aspiration, knowledge, skills, and experience to perform. Some reasons are external including at their worst: gender bias, unhealthy work situations, dysfunctional company cultures, and discrimination. There are other internal reasons like satisfaction, stress management, risk aversion, and the willingness to take on the competition.

One study of over 3,000 people reached the conclusion that women outperform men in several categories including initiative, communication, innovation, openness, sociability, supportiveness, and goal setting. The same study found that men were better at managing work-related stress. Another health care study reported that patients treated by women surgeons were less likely to die, compared to those operated on by a man. Despite this ability to outperform men, women are underrepresented in middle and senior leadership positions in corporate business, nonprofit organizations, medicine, politics, and academia. According to the Pew Research Center, women hold about 10 percent of executive leadership positions and only 11.5 percent of those positions in the next level of management.

There are many women performing in entry-level and mid-level positions every day who are exposed to all aspects of the business. Some executive administrative roles provide opportunities for short-term project leadership experiences that require a great deal of knowledge, communication, coordination, and leadership. Yet often, women in these positions are not perceived as capable of taking on a higher level role by themselves or others.

To reach a higher level position, fundamentally we all know that first and foremost, you must be willing to let people know about your interest and apply for the position. One of the most common stories told by coaches and human resources consultants who work both inside and outside organizations is the story of the super-talented woman who did not apply for the position. The reason many women say they don't apply for a position is that they feel they haven't fully mastered the skills. They also say that they thought about applying for the position, read the job description, and they felt they didn't meet all the requirements.

Many women who participated in the interviews and global survey for this book commented that women are more cautious than men when applying for a position. A couple of women told stories about men who apply for at least one job monthly or annually. The men seemed to be perfectly happy in their current positions. They applied for a new position, whether they wanted it or not, to create the perception that their skills are in demand and valuable on the job market. They also applied to learn more about the career options available to them. The fact that they did not have all the skills listed on the job description as requirements never deterred them from completing an application. Their attitudes when applying were, "I'll apply for the job because I'm interested. If I get the job, I'll learn the skills I need while I am there."

Early in her career, one woman thought of this behavior as disloyal to the employer. She always did her best in her current position, waited until she was really ready to leave a job before applying for the next position. What she realized later was that other people achieved career success because they were always open to a new career opportunity. The action of preparing a resume, keeping it up to date, and interviewing helps a person stay aware of the talent and skills she possesses. Women and men may have different perceptions of career loyalty. Women may be more deliberate when thinking about applying for a new role. They may not want to let the current team down or cause disruption at home. Men may have an easier time rationalizing that they are doing their best work in their current role, while remaining open and ready to pursue the next great opportunity.

The Globe and Mail news authority of Canada reported that women set tougher career goals than men and actually care more about them. Like New Year's resolutions, unfortunately, they said women let them slide more often than men. They interviewed the head of a development company, Mark Murphy, and uncovered a primary reason. Murphy stated that in his research findings, men were able to visualize and paint a picture of their success more clearly than women. To succeed in a role, women must be able to articulate the goal, communicate it to others, and literally see themselves as achieving it. A researcher at Monash University in Australia confirms that while women have similar career aspirations, they are less likely to expect to receive a promotion.

Finally, women must be willing to take on and be provided with challenging developmental assignments to advance. Researchers at Tilburg University found that women have fewer challenging experiences on the job than men. The act of delegation is always difficult for leaders. When the time comes for a risky assignment that may involve solving a complex business issue, dealing with a highly visible customer, or taking on a greater level of responsibility without past experience in the situation, the researchers found the leaders are more likely to delegate those assignments to men.

Susan Colantuono, CEO and founder of Leading Women, calls this factor the missing 33 percent in the career equation required for high performing women to achieve success. Colantuono says women are not lacking in leadership skills or communication. They simply aren't receiving enough coaching and experience related to business, strategic decision making, and financial acumen, according to Colantuono. Conventional coaching about developing competency strengths, overcoming weaknesses, and providing opportunities for team leadership experiences are not enough to help women advance. It takes opportunities to demonstrate the ability to think strategically and show others that you have a financial understanding of the business.

Success Strategies

Performing at a higher level than others may not be enough to advance. There are two strategies critical to advancing your career. First, you must be willing to go for it. You have to be willing to take the risk of letting go of your comfortable position. Express interest in attaining a higher level, more complex role, even if there are aspects of the new job that you have not fully mastered. You have transferable skills and must be willing to learn on the job after attaining the position.

Second, you need to complete challenging assignments that demonstrate strategic business knowledge. Ask for and volunteer for opportunities to show others that you understand the big picture. You must know how your role fits within the vision, understand financial implications, and think strategically about the future of the company.

Go for It

Apply for a job that you can learn. Many women have said, "I would love to do that job. I read the job posting and they are looking for a skill that I don't have. So, I didn't apply." Fewer women seem to say, "I saw the job posting and applied because I know I can do it. I've done something similar and I can learn." Don't settle for the position that you can perform now. Think about the position you want to hold and the skills you want to learn in the future. The worst thing that can happen when you apply for a job is that you don't get called for an interview. If you are called for an interview, you will be able to practice your interviewing skills and learn more about the role.

Look at the job posting as a wish list compiled by the employer rather than as a steadfast list. Even when the skill is listed as a requirement, if the hiring manager is unable to find a candidate possessing all the skills on the list, he may hire someone willing to learn. Be authentic and honest about your experience, but don't discount your ability to learn. Staying too long in a position without exploring other options is loyal and limiting. Be loyal to your career and continual learning, rather than to a position or company. Others may have the impression that you are not interested in learning or advancing, unable to adapt, or not willing to go beyond your comfort zone if you don't show it.

Bonnie Hagemann, CEO of Executive Development Associates, has been coaching women executives for many years. Hagemann says that she sees many women back off from applying for higher level jobs for multiple reasons. Women are collaborative so they are happy and content to continue to make a difference for the customer or company. They are more likely to agree to take on roles with less power, less credibility, and less pay than their male counterparts. While you may enjoy the current level of work and life balance in your role, her advice is to visualize rising to a higher level and even the top CEO position. Realize that when you are willing to compete for a higher level position and "take the keys" to the company, you will have more authority, more decision-making power, and more flexibility in your work life. Be intentional about your career goals, focus on your strengths, and the skills you want to learn.

Develop a supportive business network. You must be willing to let other people know about your desire and apply for a position, even if you do not feel 100 percent qualified or ready for it. When you have others in your business network, they can offer encouragement and support your application. At times, a short phone call from a trusted colleague saying, "I think you would be a great fit for the role, I think you should apply" will be enough encouragement to take that step.

Develop a business network that knows your skills, can support your interest, and lobby for you. Your career development plan should include visibility to other key stakeholders, leaders, and customers in the business. Devise a plan for networking with influential role models, both male and female. Make a list of people that have the skills you want to learn. They may be people that occupy higher level positions or people with specific skills like superior communication, project management, financial, legal, or business knowledge.

Building a business network is more than just handing out your business card or contact information. Developing strong, genuine relationships takes time. Get to know others in the same way you would develop a long-term, sincere friendship. It's a two-way relationship. Think about what you have to offer the other person as you learn from them. Women in male-dominated industries have complained about being left out of the "Good Ole Boy" networking events like the after work happy hour or Saturday golf game. This does sometimes happen, intentionally and unintentionally. It doesn't mean you need to take up golf or insert yourself in an uncomfortable situation. It does mean you should realize the importance of solid relationships at work. Sometimes a social atmosphere such as talking over lunch rather than in front of a computer helps to find a common connection and synergy away from the stress of the day-to-day tasks. Perhaps men have known this for years. They get to know each other, find common interests, and bond through after work social and athletic events. Justice Ruth Bader Ginsberg is known to have shared a love of the Opera with the late Justice Antonin Scalia. While they disagreed on many things, they developed deep respect and communication with each other.

There isn't always a clear career track from one position to another in an organization. Having colleagues that know you, are willing to help you, and have seen your talent in a variety of situations is important. As references, they can attest to the skill you demonstrated and how it might transfer to the new position.

Take on Challenging Business Assignments

Demonstrate business acumen. It's rare that you hear about a woman who rose from an administrative assistant position to CEO, but it does happen. Most often these women have taken the risk of moving laterally within a company to gain experience in several different departments. They develop a broad view of the business from working with sales associates, operations, legal, finance, and human resources. When they are given the opportunity to take the risk of managing a project related directly to business operations, demonstrate their knowledge of the company, and ability to leverage relationships, it leads to success.

Ask for challenging development assignments that are directly related to managing the operational business. Rather than just taking on more assignments within your current role, you will want to demonstrate your ability to think strategically. If you are a high performer, it will be easy to overload yourself with more responsibility related to the work you perform. Guard against this type of overload by setting boundaries and asking for critical assignments. Take a risk and take on a role that will allow you to learn more about the business. It may feel uncomfortable at first, because you may not know all the answers. One woman interviewed for this book said she was asked to be part of a strategic state-wide committee. It was an honor, but at the time she felt like an imposter surrounded by other women who were accomplished CEOs. It's important to remember that you don't need to know everything about a topic to serve on a task force. You simply need to be willing to learn, engage with others, and ask questions. Never refuse an opportunity to learn because you don't feel comfortable. Advancing your career requires getting outside of your comfort zone.

Wait for the Right Opportunity. Define the type of job you want and the way you want to be perceived by others. Women with advanced education and professional degrees are advised not to view or accept an entry-level or administrative role as a temporary alternative for entering into a company, even in a tough job market. While it may seem like a good idea to get a foot in the door, once you enter into a company it may be more difficult to advance to a higher level position quickly. Many companies have a required time frame that you must spend in your current role before applying for another position internally. There may also be limits on the maximum increase you can be given if you do apply for a higher level role. People will perceive you as an entry-level or administrative person. If it is the type of role that makes you happy and what you want for your career, be authentic. Never view it as a stepping stone to a higher level position.

Once you are inside a company, people begin to view your capability as it relates to your current position. They don't have the experience or information about the additional knowledge or experience you may bring from your past. It's more common that women in administrative "pink collar" positions are not considered as serious contenders for higher level positions within a company. While some companies are beginning to invest in sophisticated talent management systems, most still don't have the capability to inventory all your skills. Opportunities to move across functional boundaries in organizations are rare. More often people are pigeonholed into one type of role once they enter a company. It's important to be authentic and certain that you like what you will be doing once you accept a position.

Seize the Opportunity. Once the opportunity to gain experience, learn new skills, or advance that you have been waiting for presents itself, take it. Don't hesitate for any reason. It's common for a current manager to suddenly reveal how much they need you in your current position when you announce to others that you have found a new position. Counteroffers to stay are flattering, but they rarely lead to happiness. According to the *Harvard Business Review*, 80 percent of individuals who accept a counteroffer leave within 12 months. Fifty percent begin looking for another opportunity within the next 90 days. True career opportunities to learn and grow are rare. You must be ready to capitalize on them.

Assess Yourself and Plan for Development

This purpose of self-assessment is to help you enhance your effectiveness. This tool can help you chart your progress over time. It can also help you discover your strengths and development areas. Use the information to guide discussions with your manager and others in your network who can support your career development. You may also use the questions to solicit feedback from others.

Assess Yourself

Instructions: Read each question item and rate yourself on a scale of 1 to 5.

- 1 = I need serious improvement in this area.
- 2 = I need some improvement in this area.
- 3 = I'm talented and skilled in this area.
- 4 = A strength for me.
- 5 = A major strength. I consider myself a role model for other women.

Chapter 4 Assessment Questions	Rating				
1. I am willing to take the risk of accepting a job I don't yet know how to perform.	1	2	3	4	5
2. I have a list of my transferable skills that I perform well not related to my functional or technical role.	1	2	3	4	5
3. I know how my role contributes to the company's strategic vision.	1	2	3	4	5
4. I understand how the business makes money and the financial implications of my position.	1	2	3	4	5
5. I request development assignments that offer visibility and interaction across departmental boundaries.	1	2	3	4	5
6. I request development assignments that demonstrate my ability to think strategically and act with financial and business acumen.	1	2	3	4	5
7. I set boundaries to avoid task overload and willingly take on critical new assignments that allow me to learn.	1	2	3	4	5
8. I am willing to take the lead on new assignments that I have no experience performing in the past.	1	2	3	4	5
9. I perform a role that is appropriate for my capability and experience and did not settle for a lower level position.	1	2	3	4	5
10. I would not hesitate to leave a comfortable role if I was presented with a career opportunity that aligned with my goals.	1	2	3	4	5
Calculate Your Overall Average Rating					

Plan for Development

Reflect on your assessment score and plan for your future. If your overall average rating is a 4 or 5, personal presence and communication style is a strength for you. If your average rating is a 1, 2, or 3, presence and communication style could become a career derailer. On the question items where you rated yourself a 4 or 5, consider new ways to leverage your strengths. If you rated yourself a 1, 2, or 3, consider the implications for your career. These areas could get in the way of your future success. Use the ideas for leveraging strengths and developing opportunity areas to create a plan for career development.

Leverage Strengths

- Speak with others internally or externally about how your position contributes to the company's business strategy.
- Measure and share the financial implications of a project you are working on.
- Consider mentoring other women or speaking with a group of women about your career development experiences.

Develop Opportunities

- Gather information about the company's business strategy and financial performance. Assess your role and how it contributes to the company's success.
- Schedule time to meet with others within your company who perform roles outside your area of functional expertise.
- Define and volunteer for a stretch assignment, one that will stretch the boundaries of your current knowledge and experience.
- Make a list of the transferable skills you possess that you would be able to perform well in any position.
- Examine your current workload and rebalance it as needed to reduce repetitive tasks and include meaningful career development experiences.

Additional Resources

Clance, P. 1985. *The Imposter Phenomenon Overcoming the Fear that Haunts Your Success.* Atlanta, CA: Peachtree Pub Ltd.

Colantunono, S. 2013. "The Career Advice You Probably Didn't Get," *Ted Talks.* https://www.ted.com/talks/susan_colantuono_the_career_advice_you_probably_didn_t_get?utm_content=70580278

Frankel, L. 2014. *Nice Girls Don't Get the Corner Office: Unconscious Mistakes Women Make that Sabotage their Career Success.* Dublin: Business Plus.

Killelea, G. 2016. *The Confidence Effect: Every Woman's Guide to the Attitude that Attracts Success.* New York, NY: AMACOM.

Stanny, B. 2004. *Secrets of Six-Figure Women: Surprising Strategies to Up Your Earnings and Change Your Life.* New York, NY: Harper Collins Publishers.

CHAPTER 5

Myth: Women Can Expect to Be Compensated Fairly and Rewarded for Their Contributions in the Workplace

It is not fair to ask of others what you are not willing to do yourself.
—Eleanor Roosevelt

An expectation, according to the dictionary, is a strong belief, a hope, a wish, or an assumption. Most of us know the old saying about what happens when you assume—you make an ass out of you and me. Women can never expect to be compensated or rewarded fairly. There is a major difference between an expectation and an agreement. The failure to recognize the difference often leads to communication mishaps. Compensation and rewards for a job well done come only by communicating and negotiating clear agreements. Sometimes those agreements must be made with yourself.

Imagine a well-dressed, accomplished business person who has just completed the final job interview for a position that represents a significant career upward move. The phone rings and on the other end is a joyful recruiter with a job offer. This is a huge accomplishment and relief for the applicant. The interview process has included multiple steps and taken several months of preparation.

As you progress in a career, the interview process for a senior-level specialist position or leadership role can be grueling and time-consuming. Organizations are more committed than ever to getting the selection process right. They use a variety of prescreening techniques, one-on-one, group panel interviews, business assimilations, presentations, and assessments before extending an offer. When the offer comes, it's the end of the selection process, but just the beginning of the negotiation process.

Even readers of this book who are interested in the advancement of women may have imagined a man as the business person taking the call and receiving the offer at the beginning of this chapter. *The New Times* confirmed recently that multiple research studies have shown that most of us when we are asked to picture an effective leader, both men and women, usually picture a man. Getting upward career potential noticed in the workplace is more difficult for women. Taking the initiative required for pursuing a career opportunity, speaking up, and demonstrating other outwardly assertive behaviors in the workplace can come with a negative backlash for women.

Certainly intentional discrimination and unconscious gender bias play a role in the pay disparity between men and women. The Equal Employment Opportunity Commission in the United States has hundreds of complaints each year. On the other side of the globe, a research study in Australia found that women ask for raises just as often as men, but they are less likely to receive them. The overall disparity in compensation and rewards in the workplace between men and women is much more complicated than discrimination and gender bias. The researchers in Australia also found that women are more likely than men to signal their willingness to work for less.

Many women leave corporate positions and take the responsibility for owning a business with the hopes of having direct control over their own pay and rewards. Even when a woman leads her own company, researchers have found that women entrepreneurs are less likely to receive funding than male counterparts. Venture capitalists making investment decisions are more likely to ask women business owners about the potential losses associated with their businesses. Men are asked about the potential for financial gain associated with the investment in a firm.

A study in the United Kingdom found that even women entrepreneurs pay themselves approximately 29 percent less than their male entrepreneur counterparts. The women CEOs who participated in the study were responsible for setting their own pay levels and reported high career satisfaction. The study suggests that women may suffer from a paradox of being satisfied and contented at work. When women have the power to pay themselves at a level equal to their male counterparts or more, we don't always do it ourselves.

Women must not confuse job satisfaction and being content with a paycheck to the true value they bring to a position. The unique skills, talent, and position itself has a value on the job market regardless of a woman's willingness to perform the job for less. Most ambitious women are motivated by the ability to shape company culture. This was confirmed in a study by leadership research firm Korn Ferry. A sense of purpose and the desire to make a positive impact on employees, the company, or the community is a stronger driver than climbing the career ladder for increased power or pay. It's important for women to remember they deserve to be paid fairly for what they deliver.

Researching the compensation levels associated with a position and practicing good negotiation skills are essential. It's also important to have a woman as a role model. Research across international cultures confirms that women with working mothers are actually more likely to have jobs at a higher salary level than those with stay-at-home moms. Salle Yoo, an attorney for Uber, is a good example of powerful negotiation tactics. She negotiated a severance package on her way out of the company worth tens of millions of dollars. She included a clause stating that if Uber negotiated a better package with anyone else that they would match the difference. The package she finally settled upon, while a lofty sum, was less than two-thirds of her initial request.

Women can master the art of the "ask" and negotiate with practice. It also takes career opportunity, visible performance, and access to the senior-level decision makers in a large corporate environment. A study by McKinsey & Company and LeanIn.org found that women are less likely to receive challenging assignments that often lead to pay raises. They also report that women who do ask for raises and negotiate are met with bias labeling their personalities as negative, pushy, or too aggressive.

While women are now more likely than men to graduate from college, they are also more likely to choose college majors that segregate them into lower paying careers. The research conducted by Georgetown University's Center on Education and the Workforce shows as few as 8 percent women majoring in high paying fields such as mechanical engineering.

There is more encouragement for women to choose career paths previously dominated by men today and the number appears to be increasing. There are still many lower paying careers such as nursing, teaching, and child caregivers dominated by women.

Pew Research Center confirms that women are also more likely than men to say they have taken a break from a career to care for family. Career interruptions related to becoming a parent through birth or adoption or caring for a family member have a long-term impact on women's earnings. Pew reported that the women who had taken time off for family and medical leave were also twice as likely as men to say the leave had a negative impact on their careers.

The disparity in pay between women and men is a complex issue with all of these and other factors at play. Women must be encouraged to pursue high paying career roles, become skilled at negotiations based on the value of the position, and empowered to correct these gender disparities over time. Women also must take ownership for knowing the value of our work, negotiating even when we could be quite happy with less, and examining the choices we make.

Success Strategies

There are three success strategies for overcoming the complexity of issues that may interfere with your pay: know the value of your work, aim high when you negotiate, and examine the choices you make.

Know the Value of Your Work

Don't confuse satisfaction with your pay and interest in performing your work with the value of your talent on the job market. Do the research. There are a multitude of resources available with information about job titles, compensation, and benefits that can be expected both in corporate and entrepreneurial positions. Pay for the same type of professional position can also vary by industry or size of the company. It's important to gather information from industry and trade publications about the expectations based on the size and complexity of the business. Professional associations for women such as the National Association of

Women Business Owners (NAWBO) and hundreds of local Women's Business Centers supported by the Small Business Administration in the United States can offer guidance, training, and information about salary. Forbes magazine publishes a list of the best websites for women.

When you have researched the value of your position, you will be in a position to negotiate with confidence. You deserve to be paid fairly compared to others in your role, industry, and profession. It's a mistake to simply negotiate for an increase from your current pay. While you might be very well satisfied with a 10 or 15 percent increase, if you find there is a significant gap in your current pay and how the position is valued in the market, it's time to ask for more. The best employers also do this type of research annually, comparing their salary ranges with those of other companies in order to retain the best talent. For many years job applications included a place to indicate your compensation level. When extending an offer for a new position, this information was misused as a guide to the salary level for your position. Many states and countries are taking legal action to protect the confidentiality of this private information in the effort to eliminate the gender wage gap. Information about your payment history is not relevant to the value of the job. You are in a position to gather information and negotiate based on the data available and your ability to perform the work.

Aim High When You Negotiate

The Beatles said "I don't care too much for money. Money can't buy me love." It's important to love what you do, but love is only one element leading to career satisfaction. Loving what you do in a company that has an atmosphere of unethical behavior not aligned with your values just won't work. Love can also fade. You must have the opportunity to learn, the ability to contribute at a higher level, and have your skills used at their highest potential or work can be a miserable existence. Pay is not typically a satisfier. You may be in love with your job today and find out tomorrow that the new person in your department who contributes two times less than you do earns more money. Suddenly your love fades. Money is typically a dissatisfier more often than not.

Negotiate for more than you will be happy with. Keep a poker face and never signal your willingness to work for less. Gaining more money, even when you would personally be satisfied with less, gives you more to share with others, whether it is family or community. Women with the financial means can make a powerful difference in the world. Ask to see the contribution of a local Junior League if you want ideas about how to contribute. These are women dedicated to supporting local communities with their volunteerism and their money. Powerful negotiators do the research on the market value of the job. Then, they ask for much, much more—thousands of dollars more—than the target number they are willing to accept.

Never take on more job responsibilities without attempting to negotiate. The worst thing that can happen is that you receive the answer "No." Your pay stays the same and you've practiced your skills. Well-meaning busy managers often select an interim person while a position is vacant. Time flies and that interim time frame can last up to a year or more while they are searching for the right person. If it isn't you, having proven your ability to multitask, you are the only person who can make sure you get the compensation your efforts are worth.

There are many other times when organizations downsize. While you may be eager to pick up some new work that offers a real learning opportunity, evaluate the additional work you accept. Think about it's worth. Look at it in two ways—one in terms of what it does for you and your experience or to build your resume. Two, ask yourself if there is a clear business case for a raise considering the amount of extra work on your plate. Otherwise, your plate could runneth over, and there is no guarantee of anyone ever taking notice. Women sometimes find themselves in the position of taking on the work that no one else wants to do. The glass cliff phenomenon is a real problem for women who advance. Once they demonstrate the skills to obtain a position, many women are handed over a project or responsibilities that have a high probability of failure. Men often have access to more information in organizations and are better positioned to avoid a high-risk assignment.

Examine Your Own Choices

Career satisfaction is about finding a position that you have the talent to perform well in a place where you can enjoy what you do and have more than the pay you need to thrive and enjoy life outside of work. When you choose to select a major in school or accept the next offer for a new position, consider all those elements. It's not enough to take a new position because you have the talent to get the job done. If it's in a miserable environment or the pay isn't at the right level, you won't be happy in it long term. Make certain to choose positions that are the right fit for you. Ask questions about alignment in all areas—the work you will do, the people you will work with, the work environment, and the pay.

One woman who enjoyed studying psychology in school learned early on in her sophomore year by talking with other recent graduates that the pay levels were low and job opportunities were rare upon graduation. She thought about the future. She considered how many years she wanted to stay in school and the level of income she wanted to achieve upon graduation. She made a strategic decision to finish her degree, then to change majors and obtain a business degree in graduate school. By thinking strategically about her choices, she was able to create a plan that allowed her to use her knowledge of people in a business position that would bring the higher level of income she desired.

According to Forbes magazine, the young women of today could become the most financially independent women in history. We are living in a different world today compared to women in the past. Women were unable to obtain a credit card without permission from a husband in the mid 1970s. We have the freedom today to carefully consider the value of our work, negotiate for a fair salary and raises, and choose career paths that will be financially lucrative.

Assess Yourself and Plan for Development

This purpose of the self-assessment is to help you enhance your effectiveness. This tool can help you chart your progress over time. It can also help you discover your strengths and development areas. Use the information to guide discussions with your manager and others in your network who can support your career development. You may also use the questions to solicit feedback from others.

Assess Yourself

Instructions: Read each question item and rate yourself on a scale of 1 to 5.

- 1 = I need serious improvement in this area.
- 2 = I need some improvement in this area.
- 3 = I'm talented and skilled in this area.
- 4 = A strength for me.
- 5 = A major strength. I consider myself a role model for other women.

Chapter 5 Assessment Questions	Rating				
1. I research the value of a position and compensation for similar roles in the industry or regional job market before accepting an offer.	1	2	3	4	5
2. I feel comfortable asking for more money than I know will satisfy my basic living requirements.	1	2	3	4	5
3. I plan for negotiations and expect to ask for thousands of dollars more than I will receive as the final offer.	1	2	3	4	5
4. I am able to keep a straight face and avoid signaling my willingness to work for less money.	1	2	3	4	5
5. I thoroughly assess a position and its fit for me in a number of areas knowing that I will enjoy the work I perform, the people I work with, the work environment, and pay.	1	2	3	4	5
6. I am comfortable raising the topic of compensation at any time during my employment if the scope of my role changes, even for a short-term or interim assignment.	1	2	3	4	5
7. Before accepting additional responsibilities at work, I evaluate the situation fully and consider the potential impact of my choice.	1	2	3	4	5
8. I feel comfortable saying no when someone asks me to perform work that is not currently aligned with my goals or area of responsibility.	1	2	3	4	5
9. I have a long-term career plan that includes consideration about the compensation I will receive to retire comfortably in the future.	1	2	3	4	5
10. When a recruiter or hiring manager asks me about my desired compensation, I answer with a clear range based on solid business information—not an increase from my last salary.	1	2	3	4	5
Calculate Your Overall Average Rating					

Plan for Development

Reflect on your assessment score and plan for your future. If your overall average rating is a 4 or 5, personal presence and communication style is a strength for you. If your average rating is a 1, 2, or 3, presence and communication style could become a career derailer. On the question items where you rated yourself a 4 or 5, consider new ways to leverage your strengths. If you rated yourself a 1, 2, or 3, consider the implications for your career. These areas could get in the way of your future success. Use the ideas for leveraging strengths and developing opportunity areas to create a plan for career development.

Leverage strengths
- Reflect on your past success in negotiating compensation and rewards. Identify specific behaviors that worked well for you and plan to use them in the future.
- Think about the future of your career and your desired compensation levels. Create a clear plan for an enjoyable retirement that includes the monetary rewards you will receive.
- Look for an opportunity to share what you have learned about negotiating compensation and rewards with other women. It could be by developing a one-on-one mentoring relationship with another woman or by presenting to a group of women at a meeting.
- Continue to practice powerful negotiations, ask for more than you need and create a plan for sharing your wealth with others.
- Interview other successful women. Ask about how they achieved their level of success and their approach to salary negotiation.

Develop opportunities
- Reflect on your career choices and create a set of personal standards that you will not deviate from. Identify the minimum requirements that a job opportunity must meet in several areas including the work you will perform, the type of people you will work with, the work environment, and pay levels.
- Avoid signaling your willingness to work for less money or take on additional responsibilities without a discussion of pay and rewards, even for an interim or short-term assignment.

- Assess any additional responsibilities you are asked to perform carefully. Consider skills you may learn, the political environment in the situation, the hours you will work, the ability to meet your goals, and the risk of failure.
- Before accepting a new project or responsibility, consider your ability to perform the task well and the risk of saying "no." If the risk of saying "no" to the assignment is low, consider renegotiating your priorities or saying no to the request.
- Find a role model who uses powerful negotiation skills. Watch for the specific behaviors and language that work well. Incorporate those behaviors into your actions.

Additional Resources

Babcock, L., and S. Laschever. 2009. *Ask for It: How Women Can Use the Power of Negotiation to Get What They Really Want.* New York, NY: Bantam.

Babcock, L. 2007. *Women Don't Ask: The High Cost of Avoiding Negotiation and Positive Strategies for Change.* New York, NY: Bantam Dell.

Fisher, R., W. Ury, and B. Patton. 2011. "Getting to Yes: Negotiating Agreement without Giving." In *Know Your Worth, Get Your Worth: Salary Negotiation for Women,* ed. J. Olivia. New York, NY: Penguin Books.

CHAPTER 6

Myth: Men and Women Believe in Equality for Women

The history of the past is but one long struggle upward for equality.
—Elizabeth Cady Stanton

At 7:45 a.m., she walks into the lobby of the building where the business meeting will take place. The receptionist asks, "Are you here to interview for the temporary administrative assistant position?" At 8:00 a.m. the leader of the meeting arrives. He looks past her into her taller male direct report's eyes and asks, "Which one of you is the manager of this project?" At 8:15 a.m., another meeting participant looks around the room and notices her notepad. He makes eye contact with her and says, "Would you take all the notes for us?"

At 9:30 a.m., on her way out of the room, she gathers the empty coffee cups and breakfast plates on the table and throws them in the garbage can before leaving for break. At 10:00 a.m., as she walks back to the conference room a senior executive passes her in the hallway, says "Hello," and comments "Great to see you. You are always smiling." The senior executive goes into a talent review meeting at 10:30 a.m. where he debates with other leaders about her ability to handle the potential conflict associated with a new challenging project. It's almost identical to several she has delivered with ease in the past, but the customer is known to have a hot temper.

At 11:30 a.m., she leaves her meeting for lunch. She heads straight to the cafeteria where she can get a plate of food quickly and use the rest of the hour to catch up on e-mail. Her male colleagues attending the same meeting head for the parking lot together. They pile into a van and begin trading stories about the baseball game last weekend. The conversation progresses to include information about access to company-sponsored box seat tickets.

Later that afternoon, she offers an idea during the meeting that could save the company thousands of dollars. No one seemed to notice her suggestion, until another man in the meeting repeated it verbatim at 2 p.m. At 3 p.m., one of her customers holds an important meeting without her presence. The customer likes to include only people who have earned their way into his small "circle of trust." At 3:30 p.m. a senior-level woman in the meeting smiles at her, mimics the tone of her voice, and compliments her work on the project.

Her day adjourns at 5 p.m. On her way home from work, she wonders about her future career path within the company. It's been just another typical day in her life. When she interviewed for this position, they seemed impressed by her extensive experience. Now, she finds herself utterly bored with the day-to-day work and the assignments she has been given. She doesn't harbor any ill will toward the company or anyone in particular. She actually enjoys the work, likes the people, and feels she is treated pretty well by the company. She just isn't certain she has a future career path here.

While many women still encounter blatant discrimination, unconscious bias is much more common. Researchers at Rice University and the University of Memphis found the effects of unintentional bias on women are just as devastating to women's careers. Subtle behaviors directed toward a woman, such as consistently designating a woman as the note taker during meetings, while completely legal, has a long-term negative impact. The researchers argue that because women are confronted with these small behaviors on a daily or even hourly basis, the effect of this type of bias against women is compounded.

While many men and women support the advancement of women in the workplace vocally, both men and women have unconscious biases. This type of bias is hard to recognize. Sometimes it takes a crisis in which a woman is handed responsibility for a project because she is the only person available to handle it at that moment. Suddenly given the opportunity to perform, others realize she is capable of more. Writer and comedian Sarah Cooper wrote "when all else fails, wear a mustache" as the critical advice for women wanting to be taken seriously by men at work.

We are all guilty of subtle, unconscious bias. When we see a photograph of a woman and a man dressed in similar business attire, our brain gathers this information and views it in association with our past patterns. We make an immediate snap judgment. Historically, most corporate leadership positions have been held by men. If we are asked to look at pictures of a man and a woman quickly and identify which person is the leader, most of our brains almost automatically choose the man.

It seems quite irrational that women play a role in bias toward other women. Daniel Kahneman won a Nobel Prize for his work which explains the way our brain often leads us to unconscious bias. Kahneman wrote about two distinct systems we all have for thinking: System 1 and System 2. When we use System 1 thinking, we think fast and automatically. This emotional response happens quickly and instantaneously with little to no effort on our part. Our brain takes in so much information on a constant basis that it continually sifts through and sorts information. This System 1, automatic thinking, helps us survive by categorizing the overwhelming amount of data coming in.

We form unconscious bias about women simply by the information we are exposed to. There are many types of bias we may have associated with women based on our own experience. One successful woman commented that it would be hard for her to imagine a woman with a name like "Cookie" in a serious executive leadership position. We know intellectually that a person's name has little to do with qualifications and experience for a role. Many years of seeing men in powerful executive and political positions influence an unconscious reaction to women vying for those positions. System 2 thinking requires deliberate thought. It's much slower and we are more aware of the cognitive process of using analytical logic.

When asked about how many women would be enough on the Supreme Court, Justice Ruth Bader Ginsburg replied in a manner that surprised many people. "When I'm sometimes asked when will there be enough and I say, 'When there are nine,' people are shocked. But there'd been nine men, and nobody's ever raised a question about that." Reactions tell us that envisioning nine women requires deliberate thought about how they will get there.

A study by researchers at the University of Chicago found that women's own internalized sexist beliefs have a direct impact on their ability to hold powerful positions in a community. The researchers asked women in all U.S. states to respond to questions about a woman's ability to build strong relationships with family while working and to occupy a powerful position in politics like president. They ranked the states in order of the sexist attitudes prevalent among women.

When one cross-references the researchers' sexism rankings with other metrics about financial opportunities based on actual economic data, political offices held, education, and poverty indexes gathered by Wallet Hub, the impact is clear. Utah was ranked as the worst state for gender equality across 16 indicators including unemployment and the gap in executive level positions. By comparison, Utah was ranked as the second most gender-biased state by the researchers at the University of Chicago.

Even more interesting, the researchers found that the state in which a woman is born affects her financial outcomes, even when she is an adult living in another less sexist market. This seems to validate the influence of our unconscious bias that is learned in early years of childhood. We must all increase our self-awareness to understand and address the impact of unconscious bias. We can only overcome unintentional discriminatory behaviors when we know of them and take action.

Success Strategies

There are two success strategies for overcoming the impact of unconscious bias. First, we must all take responsibility and increase our own self-awareness. Then, we must recognize our own biases and make decisions with clear criteria to neutralize the impact.

Self-Awareness

Knowing about bias intellectually and reflecting on our own bias are two different things. Reflecting on our own bias and the impact it has on our perceptions of others in the workplace is the first step in addressing it. Professor Shelley Corell at Stanford University says we often have narrow perceptions of what a leader should be like that overlap with our stereotypes about men. When we recognize this type of bias, we can make a conscious effort to broaden our definition of effective leadership behavior. Until you are able to see the biases and stereotypes you hold about gender and specific job-related roles in an organization, you will be unable to take action to overcome them.

Once we become aware of our own bias, we can influence others with our example. Women who have made broad statements indicating fear about supporting the career advancement of women to senior leadership levels can begin to support the advancement of other women openly. It requires letting go of the perception that the number of seats for women are limited and that another woman represents competition for my position at the top. Biases about feminine sounding names and abilities can be addressed.

There are many ways to reflect on biases we hold. You might think about the beliefs you have about gender and career. You might think about keywords such as leader, emotional, caring, and strong and notice the relationship they have in your mind to gender. You might also practice careful observation about the conversations that take place in your work environment related to women and their capabilities. When you notice the specific differences in the way women and men's capabilities are described in your workplace, you can then speak with confidence about your ideas for ensuring decisions impacting people are approached with fairness.

Approach Decisions with a Clear Criteria

All people in an organization have influence regardless of their formal title or position. People at all levels move projects forward, work with others to make decisions, and lead improvement efforts. Depending on your role in an organization, you may have more authority for decision making related to hiring, promotions, career development, and performance reviews. Regardless of the type of decision you are making, it's important to approach it with fairness and a clear criteria. Without a clearly defined decision-making criteria, we leave it to chance for our unconscious bias to creep in and impact the outcome.

Korn Ferry, a leading organizational development firm, recommends using a diverse interview team and objective selection criteria, such as nameless resumes and psychometric testing, to ensure hiring and promotion decisions are being made without bias. For an everyday project related decision, taking the time to solicit the input from a team of diverse stakeholders who will be impacted by it can also have merit.

It could be a brief team meeting in which key stakeholders agree on the "must have," "nice to have," and "not required" criteria for the final project. This simple step can help eliminate situations in which the final product completed by a woman could be perceived differently than the project if it were completed by a man. When we clarify and agree with others about what a successful outcome looks like in advance, it's easier to gain support from others and evaluate success. When you consciously use analytical thinking techniques, you engage System 2 thinking, slow the process down, and avoid making an immediate decision based on assumptions.

Assess Yourself and Plan for Development

This purpose of the self-assessment is to help you enhance your effectiveness. This tool can help you chart your progress over time. It can also help you discover your strengths and development areas. Use the information to guide discussions with your manager and others in your network who can support your career development. You may also use the questions to solicit feedback from others.

Assess Yourself

Instructions: Read each question item and rate yourself on a scale of 1 to 5.

- 1 = I need serious improvement in this area.
- 2 = I need some improvement in this area.

- 3 = I'm talented and skilled in this area.
- 4 = A strength for me.
- 5 = A major strength. I consider myself a role model for other women.

Chapter 6 Assessment Questions	Rating				
1. I have a broad view of leadership that includes both stereotypical masculine and feminine qualities.	1	2	3	4	5
2. I actively support the career advancement of other women in my workplace.	1	2	3	4	5
3. I believe there are an unlimited number of seats for women in higher level positions in an organization.	1	2	3	4	5
4. I am cautious about making quick decisions about the ability of a person.	1	2	3	4	5
5. I approach decisions with a clear criteria in mind to ensure the outcome is fair.	1	2	3	4	5
6. I take the time to solicit input on decisions and change in the workplace from a diverse group of stakeholders.	1	2	3	4	5
7. I clarify specific decision-making criteria and discuss the elements of a successful outcome before reaching agreements with others.	1	2	3	4	5
8. I have reflected on my own biases and understand how they might influence my behavior and decisions at work.	1	2	3	4	5
9. I speak up to eliminate bias in the workplace when I observe subtle differences in the way men and women are treated.	1	2	3	4	5
10. I use gender-neutral language and decision-making methods such as nameless resumes for selection or project evaluations.	1	2	3	4	5
Calculate Your Overall Average Rating					

Plan for Development

Reflect on your assessment score and plan for your future. If your overall average rating is a 4 or 5, personal presence and communication style is a strength for you. If your average rating is a 1, 2, or 3, presence and communication style could become a career derailer. On the question items where you rated yourself a 4 or 5, consider new ways to leverage your strengths. If you rated yourself a 1, 2, or 3, consider the implications for your career. These areas could get in the way of your future success. Use the ideas for leveraging strengths and developing opportunity areas to create a plan for career development.

Leverage strengths
- Find ways to educate others and increase the awareness of unconscious bias in your workplace.
- Volunteer to facilitate a discussion about actions you can take to improve decision making, using analytical techniques that help eliminate bias.
- Have a discussion with a woman about career development. Offer to share your knowledge or introduce this woman to key people in your network.
- Encourage others in your workplace to adopt gender-neutral language and diverse photographs when presenting information to others.
- When you notice signs of unconscious bias, stop in the moment and share your observations with others. Then offer an alternative. It may be simply stating a fact such as, "I noticed the woman in our meeting seems to always takes the notes. I'd like to offer to record them today."

Develop opportunities
- Slow down, observe, and reflect your own daily behavior. Identify decisions and actions you take that may have unconscious bias toward others.
- Identify a diverse set of key stakeholders and ask for their input prior to making decisions that will affect them.
- Before making a final decision, write down the outcome you want to achieve and ensure you have a clear criteria for selecting your path forward.
- Reflect on your past behavior and decisions that may have been influenced by unconscious bias. Set specific goals for improvement.
- Observe the interactions between people in your workplace and listen for signs of unconscious bias. Identify ways to build better relationships and foster a more inclusive environment.

Additional Resources

Banaji, M., and A. Greenwald. 2016. *Blindspot: Hidden Biases of Good People*. New York, NY: Random House Publishing Group.

Bohnet, I. 2016. *What Works: Gender Equality by Design*. Cambridge, MA: Harvard University Press.

Brown, J. 2017. *Inclusion: Diversity, the New Workplace and the Will to Change*. Charleston, SC: Advantage Media Group.

Crawford, J. 2015. "Webstock '15 Janet Crawford "The Surprising Neuroscience of Gender Inequality," *Vemo Video*. https://vimeo.com/124887217

Gladwell, M. 2007. *Blink: The Power of Thinking without Thinking*. Boston, MA: Back Bay Books.

Kahneman, D. 2013. *Thinking Fast and Slow*. New York, NY: Farrar, Straus and Giroux.

CHAPTER 7

Myth: Women Can Have It All—Work and Life Balance

You can't have everything that you want, but you can have the things that really matter to you.

—Marissa Mayer

As director of policy planning for the U.S. State Department, Anne-Marie Slaughter once wrote in an essay for *The Atlantic* that she thought she had a foreign policy dream job, one that she would stick to as long as she had the career opportunity. Ultimately, she gave up her dream position and returned to academia. She lived in Washington, D.C. during the week and went home on weekends to be with her husband and children in New Jersey. When she accepted the government job, she began working long hours on someone else's schedule.

She caught a 5:30 a.m. train from New Jersey to Washington on Mondays and worked long hours each day, ending the workweek late on Fridays. Even with understanding bosses and a supportive husband who took on the lion's share of parenting during her stint at the State Department, Slaughter wrote, she could no longer be both the parent and the professional she wanted to be. With one of her sons experiencing a rocky adolescence, she decided it was not possible to juggle the high-level government work with the needs of her children.

In leaving the State Department, Slaughter also gave up her belief that women could have it all regardless of their profession. "I realized what should have perhaps been obvious: having it all, at least for me, depended almost entirely on what type of job I had. The flip side is the harder truth: having it all was not possible in many types of jobs, including high government office—at least not for very long," Slaughter said in the essay.

Many working women, like Slaughter, are surprised at some point in their careers by the harsh reality of balancing work responsibilities with their personal lives. A LinkedIn study of thousands of working women around the world shows that work–life balance is important to us. Nearly two-thirds of the women who responded say they view career success as achieving that balance. Seventy-four percent of the more than 5,300 respondents said they thought it was true that they could have it all—a fulfilling career, a relationship, and children.

The growth and reliance on technology has blurred the line between our work and home life. Some women may feel comfortable responding to work phone calls or e-mails while vacationing on the beach in Mexico. Others may feel a sense of guilt for leaving the work phone behind or the sense that they may miss out on an important message that could be a disadvantage at work. While some companies and positions offer flexible work hours and options such as working from home, studies show women still have challenges in achieving balance between work and life.

According to a report by the National Alliance for Caregiving, women are still the primary caregivers for children and ill family members and two out of three are employed outside the home. Another study from UCLA says that while the primary childcare time of both mothers and fathers at home has risen, parents still report having too little time with their children. Women also frequently experience job spillover into the home, according to Women's Health Issues. This is more common than personal responsibilities creeping into the workplace. Women typically shoulder more of the childcare responsibilities and handle more household demands than men. A Pew Research study found that while the traditional roles of women and men are converging, 56 percent of women with children still find it stressful to juggle work and home life.

The difficulty of achieving that vision of career success with the perfect balance between work and life affects working women everywhere. An association president in California said that even when a woman is in what is considered an equal partnership with a man, she believes most women will still have the bigger role in raising children. An executive in Germany said she was surprised by how much her professional male colleagues at work depended on their wives. The men could have it all because the women in their life, even if they had a job, still made all the meals and cared for the children. They also took on the traditionally fe-male tasks at home, like cleaning the house.

In the United Kingdom, a CEO said she believed it was possible to put in the hours necessary at the office to rise through the ranks, as well as spend plenty of time with her family. But when her children were born, the executive believed she should not take the 12-month maternity leave that was customary in the UK and instead returned to work in 6 weeks. She then felt guilty about not being with her kids as often as she would have liked. In the long term, she knew that her children were not harmed at all by her decision to return to work quickly after giving birth.

Indra Nooyi, the former CEO of PepsiCo, told a similar story when she was interviewed by David Bradly, owner of *The Atlantic*. Nooyi said, "I don't think women can have it all. I just don't think so. We pretend we *have* it all. We pretend we *can* have it all. . .And every day you have to make a decision about whether you are going to be a wife or a mother, in fact many times during the day you have to make those decisions." Like the woman in the UK, Nooyi was not certain her children would feel she has been a good mother. The opposite was true; the woman in the UK discovered that her grown daughter viewed her as a positive role model—exactly what a working mother should look like.

Emotional guilt may be the culprit that prevents many women from ever feeling work and life are balanced. Women are still expected to be the primary caregiver at home. A Harvard Business Review study of inter-views collected over 5 years with approximately 4,000 executives confirms that both women and men believe the dilemma of how to manage stress between work and family is primarily an issue for women, not men.

This dilemma is not one that single, childless women are immune to by any means. A study at Michigan State University confirmed that work–life balance isn't just about how a woman chooses to juggle work and a family. It is also about how a single working woman is able to find balance between work responsibilities and time for interests outside of a professional career. In the MSU study, researchers found many people suffer from stress due to the inability to find time for leisure activities such as working out at the gym, vol-unteering in the community, or spending enough quality time with friends.

Cassie Murdoch wrote about the way single women view this issue of obtaining the perfect work–life balance. She referenced a survey in which

68 percent of childless women professionals say they would prefer having more time off than more pay. Murdoch also wrote about a study of working women at 60 companies conducted by McKinsey & Company. The study found both working mothers and single childless women were planning to leave their jobs because they had a desire for "more control over their personal schedules."

Work–life balance may mean having enough time to spend with and care for the dog, according to Emily Van Zandt, a writer for the *Washington Business Journal*. More professional women are choosing to stay unmarried and making the decision not to have children today. Yet, she references a study in the UK by PricewaterhouseCoopers that confirms that the majority of women without kids between the ages of 28 and 40 feel pressured at the office to work longer hours than their colleagues with children.

Many factors make our ideal image of a great career with the perfect balance between work and life difficult to achieve. The struggle to balance work and life may continue to be a growing issue for women and men. A global study by Ernst and Young found that the Millennial Generation is almost twice as likely to have a spouse or partner who is working fulltime and at least one-third of workers say it is getting more difficult to manage work and life outside the office. Even when a woman has a great career, a family, children, a caring husband, a cute fluffy dog or cat, and good friends, she still might not feel like she has it all. It may be more important to decide what really matters most to you.

Success Strategies

There are four strategies for overcoming this myth. First, you must know and live your values. Then discuss your life plans with others and always be ready to prioritize. Finally, look for flexible work options.

Know and Live Your Values

In the classic comedy City Slickers, Curly the cowboy gives us the secret of life. He holds up a finger and says you have to know one thing. When asked what it is, he says, "That's what you've got to figure out." It is important for you to have a vision for your own life. Stop and think about your personal values and let them guide your behavior. Some of us value time with family above everything else. Others value high achievement at work or leaving a legacy of meaningful work for others. Often people get caught up in day-to-day life and feel stressed when the demands of work collide with personal time. When you have taken the time to define your values and know what is most important to you, it will be easier to make decisions when work and life responsibilities conflict.

There are a number of values assessments and sorting cards available to help define your own set of values. They typically have a predefined list of items such as loyalty, innovation, independence, creativity, and adventure. There isn't one right or wrong answer; like Curly's advice, you have to figure out what is most important to you. Then, if your family reunion occurs at the same time that you are offered the challenging work assignment you have been yearning for, you will be able to let your values guide the decision you make.

Discuss Life Plans with Partners

If you are married or in a relationship, talk to your partner about your values and life plans. Andrea Lekushoff, president of Broad Reach Communications, suggested in a *Huffington Post* blog that discussions with your partner should include the decision to have children; responsibilities for caring for aging parents; any plans to go back to school; and how you will manage the demands of work. The conversation should clarify how you and your partner will share responsibilities at home and care for family. You will want to be very clear about whether one or both of you will work and how career choices will be made.

Set Priorities

Women must always be ready and able to prioritize. They must be able to decide what they want and when they want it, in both their personal and professional lives. Women also need to keep in mind that priorities can change during different times of life. Employees starting out might work more hours to launch their careers, but then switch to part-time when they start a family or need to take care of an ill family member. Later, they may want to take a year off to go back to school. While our values usually remain constant, priorities can shift depending on the circumstances around us.

Look for Flexible Work Options

With priorities in mind, look for a job that allows the time for a life outside work. Many employers are realizing that flexibility can help employees achieve a better work–life balance. When job hunting, ask about the company's work demands and policies on flex hours, telecommuting, or working from home. Being able to work from home at night or from home during the day when a child is sick can help women get their work done while juggling family responsibilities.

Even if you already have a job, it is worth thinking creatively about how you might be able to get work done outside the typical 8-to-12 hour day in an office. It may be worth raising the issue of flexible options with your employer. Sometimes small changes to work routines can make a huge difference. Using technology like videoconferencing, Skype, WebEx, or other techniques to perform the work can reduce travel expenses for a company while allowing time at home.

According to the Society of Human Resources Management, over half of the HR professionals surveyed say that flexible work arrangements that include options such as compressed work weeks, flexible shift start times, telecommuting, and casual dress are having a positive impact on business operations. Propose an idea that will increase your personal work–life satisfaction and have a positive impact on a company's success.

Assess Yourself and Plan for Development

This purpose of self-assessment is to help you enhance your effectiveness. This tool can help you chart your progress over time. It can also help you discover your strengths and development areas. Use the information to guide discussions with your manager and others in your network who can support your career development. You may also use the questions to solicit feedback from others.

Assess Yourself

Instructions: Read each question item and rate yourself on a scale of 1 to 5.

- 1 = I need serious improvement in this area.
- 2 = I need some improvement in this area.
- 3 = I'm talented and skilled in this area.
- 4 = A strength for me.
- 5 = A major strength. I consider myself a role model for other women.

Chapter 7 Assessment	Rating				
1. I have clearly defined my values and use them to guide directions.	1	2	3	4	5
2. The choices I have made when work and life responsibility conflict are in alignment with the value most important to me.	1	2	3	4	5
3. I have discussed my life plans with my spouse, partner, or others important to me.	1	2	3	4	5
4. I have had detailed discussions with others about choices I may need to make in the future about my career, caring for family, continued education, or other life decisions.	1	2	3	4	5
5. I am ready and able to prioritize work and life responsibility, rather than reacting to the situation in ways I might regret later.	1	2	3	4	5
6. When searching for a new career opportunity, I ask about the company's policy for flexible work arrangements.	1	2	3	4	5
7. I raise creative ideas for working that will increase my personal satisfaction and have a positive impact on business performance.	1	2	3	4	5
8. I know what is most important to me when attempting to balance work and life outside my career.	1	2	3	4	5
9. I have no emotional guilt or regrets about choices I have made in the past about work and home or family.	1	2	3	4	5
10. I feel confident about handling future decisions when my work or career decisions conflict with the needs of my spouse, partner, family or others in my life.	1	2	3	4	5
Calculate Your Overall Average Rating					

Plan for Development

Reflect on your assessment score and plan for your future. If your overall average rating is a 4 or 5, personal presence and communication style is a strength for you. If your average rating is a 1, 2, or 3, presence and communication style could become a career derailer. On the question items where you rated yourself a 4 or 5, consider new ways to leverage your strengths. If you rated yourself a 1, 2, or 3, consider the implications for your career. These areas could get in the way of your future success. Use the ideas for leveraging strengths and developing opportunity areas to create a plan for career development.

Leverage strengths
- Lead a discussion with others at work about how you balance your work and life responsibilities.
- Mentor a woman at work and have open dialogue about conflicts that may arise between work and home.
- Share your personal values with others and explain how you use them to guide your life choices and behavior.
- Volunteer to lead a committee empowered to research, identify, and propose new flexible work options that will increase employee satisfaction and positively impact business performance.
- Express gratitude for others, whether it is a manager, spouse, or partner, who support the balance of your career and personal life.

Develop opportunities
- Assess or write your personal values and share them with others who know you well. Ask for feedback on your behavior and it's alignment to them.
- Discuss your life plans with your spouse, partner, or others in your life who can support them.
- When you experience a conflict between work and home, react calmly, consider the situation, and prioritize what is most important to you now.
- Let go of emotional guilt about career and work decisions you have made that may have had a negative impact on your life outside of work.
- Brainstorm a list of actions that you can take to improve your satisfaction with work and life. Include any options for flexible work that may be supported by your employer.

Additional Resources

De Graaf, J. 2012. *Take Back Your Time: Fighting Overwork and Time Poverty in America.* San Francisco, CA: Berrett-Koehler Publishers.

Heath, C., and D. Heath. 2013. *Decisive: How to Make Better Choices in Life and Work.* New York, NY: Crown Business.

Kouzes, J. M., and B. Z. Pozner. *The Leadership Challenge Workshop: Values Cards.* Hoboken, NJ: John Wiley & Sons, Inc.

Sandberg, S. 2013. *Lean In: Women, Work, and the Will to Lead.* New York, NY: Alfred A. Knopf.

Slaughter, A. 2016. *Unfinished Business: Women, Men, Work, Family.* London, England: Oneworld Publications.

CHAPTER 8

Myth: Women Are Supportive of Each Other, Men Compete

There is a special place in hell for women that don't help other women.
—Madeleine Albright

Many women get excited about the idea of working with other successful women. They think about how nice it will be to have someone like them as a role model or even a mentor. They might even assume another woman in the office will be more empathetic, understanding the barriers that women face in the workplace. It isn't always so. Talk with any group of women and you will find that almost every woman has a story to tell about a "queen bee" or "mean girl" they have had to navigate working with.

She's the one who seems to enjoy bullying the other women in the office. She gossips about her female coworkers behind their backs and demeans them to their faces at meetings—that is, if she hasn't "forgotten" to tell them they were supposed to attend the meeting. She rolls her eyes, makes sarcastic remarks, never misses an opportunity to point out a real or an imaginary mistake. As a manager, she assigns way more work than could possibly be done in the time allotted and is always on the lookout for a way to sabotage another woman's career. Whether you call her a queen bee or a mean girl, she makes other women miserable, impedes their careers, and costs her employer money. She proves, through her bullying and incivility, that the belief that women support each other is indeed a myth.

The queen bee syndrome was first defined in 1973 by psychologists at the University of Michigan as a woman in a position of authority in a male-dominated industry who treats colleagues and subordinates more critically if they are female. Another definition refers to a queen bee as someone who has succeeded in her career but won't support the advancement of other women. A successful woman speaking on a panel of women encountered one who openly admitted it. She was in shocked disbelief hearing her professional colleague say, "I'm not going to support other women's career advancement. I am holding the one seat in my company at the executive table that is there for a woman."

London-based consultant Cecilia Harvey, the founder and chair of global showcase platform Tech Women Today, describes queen bees as versions of the mean girls from school who have grown up and are now more calculating. The phenomenon starts in middle school or in high school, when some girls form cliques and exclude other girls from their social circle. The queen bee or mean girl has been portrayed in movies, including *Mean Girls* and *Heathers*. A study by Harvey showed that 70 percent of female executives felt they had been bullied by other women in the workplace. Queen bees should not be confused with strong, ambitious women in the workplace, Harvey said.

It makes one wonder what could cause the phenomenon of women discriminating against other women. There are many theories. One theory is that the powerful women may deal with sexism in the workplace by distancing themselves from other females. This way they can show masculine qualities that are stereotypically considered more valuable in the workplace. Some women in male-dominated industries may believe their company has only so many spots for female executives. They must fight other women for the "token female" job. Other women fear being accused of bias if they help women. Those who had to fight their way to the top might feel resentful if a female coworker seems to have an easier time of it.

Yet another theory says that evolution plays a part in the behavior and that women undermine one another because they have always had to compete for mates and resources for their offspring. Dr. Nancy O'Reilly, a licensed psychologist, writes that the way female apes will often attack other females to survive and befriend a powerful male is not unlike women knocking other women off the career ladder. Joyce Benenson, a psychologist at Emmanuel College agrees writing that male chimpanzees will work together, groom one another, and hunt together, while female apes are less likely to do so. Her research suggests that women are more likely to socially exclude other women and dissolve same gender friendships. Not all researchers agree that the queen bee phenomenon actually exists.

Still there are stories that persist of women who believe their careers have suffered because of another woman. Many of the women who responded anonymously to the survey for this book provided comments about how "women can be the worst! We are sometimes best at being petty, catty, and manipulative." They said, "women are more aggressive than men toward other women." One respondent wrote," Sadly, the reality is that my biggest obstacles and attempted derailments have come from other women throughout my career. This truth is devastating to the careers of many women."

One woman said, "I can't quite figure out if it's because women feel so insecure in their leadership roles, or that they play out the way they were treated in getting to their positions, or it's the unsympathetic and down-right mean women who make it to those positions. I know this will not be a popular comment, but I know I am not the only one who has had these experiences. While I find that women are more open to new ideas, I've also found them to be exceptionally unforgiving and mean."

Another respondent suggested that "women may expect more of other women. I have, unfortunately, found that many women sabotage other women in their area, citing issues such as child care, children who are ill, as well as a multitude of other things, and they are rougher on other females instead of being understanding." Yet another stated, "Women can judge harshly a woman who is not handing a challenge as well as someone else or handling it in a different way."

The stories suggest that the aggressive tactics used by women are more subtle, difficult to identify, and almost impossible to address compared to obvious discrimination or some of the ways men might try to coerce others. "The bullying of women by other women is a major issue which seems to go unmentioned for some reason. Women's bullying of women has actively forced out women from jobs and career paths and is some-thing that we need to admit to and deal with. For example, it is far easier to remove a man from a role if he is bullying because he will do something obvious, like punch a wall, but to get rid of a female bullying is almost impossible. HR policies are set up to deal with male violence (physical) versus female violence (verbal)." They used the term "womenemy" and said, "Above all, stop talking about others and passing judgment. Trash talking and lack of trust give birth to career killing."

Harvey, citing the Workplace Bullying Institute, says that 58 percent of bullies in the workplace are female and that nearly 90 percent of their victims were other women. According to the *Harvard Business Review*, women engage in more subtle bullying behavior than men, with nearly 54 percent using sabotage and about 50 percent using abuse of authority. A trio of studies at the University of Arizona took a look at the issue, asking women and men about the incivility and rudeness that they had experienced in the workplace. Participants were asked about coworkers who put them down or were condescending, made demeaning or derogatory remarks, ignored them in a meeting, or addressed them in unprofessional terms. Each set of questions was answered once for male coworkers and once for female coworkers.

"Across the three studies, we found consistent evidence that women reported higher levels of incivility from other women than their male counterparts," said Allison Gabriel, assistant professor of management and organizations in the University of Arizona's Eller College of Management. In a news release, she stated, "In other words, women are ruder to each other than they are to men, or than men are to women."

The research study also showed that the women who defied gender norms by being more assertive and dominant at work were more likely to be targeted by their female counterparts. This may mean that you are more likely to be sabotaged than supported by other women when you show assertiveness, perform well, and begin to advance at work.

In an article for *The New York Times*, Sheryl Sandberg pointed out that women can still pay a price when they advocate for other women. She wrote about a story of 300 executives that showed when men promoted diversity, they received slightly higher performance ratings. When women executives promoted diversity, they received significantly lower performance ratings. As Sandberg said in the article, it is about time for us to show that "Women can disagree—even compete—and still have one another's backs."

Success Strategies

There are three strategies for overcoming this myth—protect yourself, just stop it, and always perform to the best of your ability.

Protect Yourself

Think bee repellent. If you think about bees—the flying insects, it really hurts when they sting. They can be quite pesky, difficult to handle, and hard to get rid of. They may even have a swarm of others ready to charge out of a nest and attack for them. If you Google home improvement you can find any number of do-it-yourself bee repellent remedies. Doityourself.com advises, "While your first instinct might be to kill hornets with harsh chemicals, there are ways to rid them from your home in a more natural way." It's the essentially same advice for handling the queen bee woman. While you may be angry enough to attack, it's rarely worth launching a counterattack for one moment of satisfaction. Defensive or protective strategies are most likely to protect your reputation and career.

Remember, you must be aware of the signs of subtle sabotage. Women are more likely to use less obvious bullying tactics. Never assume because a coworker or a manager is a woman that they will be empathetic to you as a woman or support your career. According to Business Insider, some signs that you are being undermined at work include colleagues gossiping about you or others, leaving you out of meetings, giving you incomplete information about a project, taking credit for work you performed, and not inviting you to social events. Another sign is that plain old gut feeling you get when there is some deception happening. Some women who use these tactics actually will do it quite openly if they believe they have enough power in the organization to get away with it.

One woman who worked for a successful woman in a Vice President role spent hours writing a strategic planning document that her boss urgently needed for a meeting. After the VP received the information, she made it clear that she would present the plan to others as if she had written it alone. She asked her direct report in a meeting, "Would you like to see my plan?" Then shared the identical document with her employee in a subtle but intimidating tone. A defensive and repelling strategy that works in a situation like this is to simply guard the amount of information you are willing to share.

While the VP was able to present the overall plan as hers to others, her direct report knew that the VP would not be able to answer detailed questions about how the plan would be implemented without her involvement. It is true that your role as an employee is to help your manager look good. You must be willing to roll up your sleeves to help the team and the company in a situation like this, but you must also watch for subtle subterfuge and protect your own career too. Both parties can succeed if the overall presentation of strategy goes well and if your role as critical to implementation is known. The best leaders and managers know this and they willingly give credit to others for their work.

You might also make an effort to build a relationship or show interest in her success. This does not always work, but there are some who believe you can kill the queen bee with kindness. There is an old saying, spoken by Michael Corleone in the movie *The Godfather*, "Keep your friends close, and your enemies closer." The queen bee or mean girl may never change her evil ways. If you can earn some level of trust and use good listening skills, she may let you in on some of her plans. It is better to be informed of her evil plans directed toward others than to be the unknowing target of them. Consider confronting or reporting her behavior only when it is unavoidable for ethical or procedural violations. Just like the bees in the hive, when confronted she and others may attack.

Just Stop It

Most likely, if you are reading this book, you are not one of those queen bee or grown up mean girl women. Even so, consider the words of Mahatma Gandhi, "You must be the change you wish to see in the world." There is an opportunity for every woman to show others how to treat women in the workplace. Think about your own behavior in the workplace and the actions you have taken to show support for other women. Reflect on the level of civility you show to other women, compared to men. Examine your own behavior and make sure you aren't inadvertently undermining another woman.

Yes, it could happen accidently. You don't want to be perceived as the rude, uncaring, queen bee, or mean girl in your office. Perhaps you talked over another more introverted woman in a meeting. Being disliked by other women is not good for your career. Another example might be moving forward with a project that overlaps in some way with another woman's responsibility area. Consider your role, your responsibilities, and key stakeholders that should be involved in your plans. Involve other women, reach out to mentor them, support their contribution, and show recognition for their ideas. We have to set the example for others to follow.

We also have to stop judging women's behavior more harshly than men. Some women will be more driven and competitive than others. Just like some men are more assertive and competitive than others. In the world of work, some level competition is healthy. Everyone is there to contribute to the company's overall performance by achieving goals. If another woman is honestly having a bad day and is inadvertently rude, don't take it too personally. Don't engage in gossip about other women. When another woman succeeds, celebrate it.

Always Perform Your Best

When it comes to guiding your career forward, the one thing you can do regardless of the behavior directed toward you is always perform to the best of your ability. You will never be able to control the queen bee or mean girl's behavior. You can only control how you respond to it. Always keep your emotions in check and respond professionally. In the worst case scenario, you will leave the position to find another one in a more civil and enjoyable environment. As you are interviewing for your next position, you will want to talk about what you have learned in your position and your accomplishments. There are companies today owned by women who are committed to providing career opportunities for other women. There are companies owned by men and male-dominated industries committed to the advancement of women. When you perform to the best of your ability, there is always a path forward even if it means leaving the current hive.

Assess Yourself and Plan for Development

This purpose of self-assessment is to help you enhance your effectiveness. This tool can help you chart your progress over time. It can also help you discover your strengths and development areas. Use the information to guide discussions with your manager and others in your network who can support your career development. You may also use the questions to solicit feedback from others.

Assess Yourself

Instructions: Read each question item and rate yourself on a scale of 1 to 5.

- 1 = I need serious improvement in this area.
- 2 = I need some improvement in this area.
- 3 = I'm talented and skilled in this area.
- 4 = A strength for me.
- 5 = A major strength. I consider myself a role model for other women.

Chapter 8 Assessment	Rating				
1. I pay attention and recognize subtle warning signs that women are undermining other women in the workplace.	1	2	3	4	5
2. I am able to protect my work by sharing an appropriate level of information with others that supports their goals and my career.	1	2	3	4	5
3. I show respect and support other women in the office even when their goals may compete with my own.	1	2	3	4	5
4. I manage my emotions and speak up in a professional manner if I am left out of a discussion or project in which I should have been included.	1	2	3	4	5
5. I could maintain a relationship with a queen bee or a mean girl without engaging in any unethical or nasty behavior toward others.	1	2	3	4	5
6. I expect women in the workplace to exhibit assertive or competitive behavior and don't judge them more harshly than men for it.	1	2	3	4	5
7. I set an example for others by involving women in my work and recognizing their ideas.	1	2	3	4	5
8. I know that a bully at work is unlikely to change her behavior and look for ways to protect my career, which may mean leaving for another job.	1	2	3	4	5
9. Even when I don't have all the information, I listen to my gut feeling about deception at work and take action to guard against harm to my career.	1	2	3	4	5
10. I am able to stay focused on my performance and achieve high results even in a difficult situation—working with others that don't support my career.	1	2	3	4	5
Calculate Your Overall Average Rating					

Plan for Development

Reflect on your assessment score and plan for your future. If your overall average rating is a 4 or 5, personal presence and communication style is a strength for you. If your average rating is a 1, 2, or 3, presence and communication style could become a career derailer. On the question items where you rated yourself a 4 or 5, consider new ways to leverage your strengths. If you rated yourself a 1, 2, or 3, consider the implications for your career. These areas could get in the way of your future success. Use the ideas for leveraging strengths and developing opportunity areas to create a plan for career development.

Leverage strengths
- Lead a discussion about how to navigate politics in the office with ethical defense strategies.
- Recognize the women in the workplace who support the careers of other women.
- Coach another woman about how to build productive relationship with difficult coworkers.
- Make it known to others that you will not tolerate tactics like leaving others out of meetings, gossiping, or taking credit for someone else's work.
- Share a story about how you were able to successfully work with a queen bee or mean girl for others to learn from. Include how you managed your own career interests in the situation and dealt with the offensive behavior.

Develop opportunities
- Discuss how your work team(s) will operate and set guidelines for appropriate behavior when working together.
- Focus on managing anger or negative emotions about others who behave badly. Instead, build a working relationship with them that will benefit your own career.
- Reflect on your engagement and satisfaction at work. If the people in your work environment are unbearable, consider looking for a new position.

- Reflect on your own behavior and make changes necessary to ensure you are not inadvertently undermining other women.
- Create a list of your work accomplishments and share it with others who can support your career at work.

Additional Resources

Crowley, K., and K. Elster. 2007. *Working with You is Killing Me: Freeing Yourself from Emotional Traps at Work.* New York, NY: Warner Business.

Crowley, K., and K. Elster. 2012. *Mean Girls at Work: How to Stay Professional When Things Get Personal.* New York, NY: McGraw-Hill Education.

Davenport, N., and R. D. Schwartz, G. P. Elliott. 1999. *Mobbing: Emotional Abuse in the American Workplace.* Ames, IA: Civil Society Pub.

Dellasega, C. 2007. *Mean Girls Grown Up: Adult Women Who Are Still Queen Bees, Middle Bees, and Afraid-to-Bees.* Hoboken, NJ: John Wiley & Sons, Inc.

Dillon, K. 2014. *HBR Guide to Office Politics.* Boston, MA: Harvard Business Review.

Namie, G., and R. Namie. 2009. *The Bully at Work: What You Can Do to Stop the Hurt and Reclaim Your Dignity on the Job.* Naperville, IL: Sourcebooks.

CHAPTER 9

Myth: Both Men and Women Are Perceived as Equally Effective Leaders

If more women are in leadership roles, we'll stop assuming they shouldn't be.

—Sheryl Sandberg

"Okay, she's tough, but if Miranda were a man no one would notice anything about her, except how great she is at her job," says Andy Sachs the fictional assistant in the movie *The Devil Wears Prada*. The movie is a comedy about working for a boss from Hell based on a best selling novel by the same name. It is fiction, but according to Laura Weisberger, the author, many of the scenes are based on her own experiences working for *Vogue* magazine's editor-in-chief Anna Wintour and the experiences of other friends.

It's fun to watch Miranda Priestly's sarcasm, biting comments, and lack of concern for the people who work for her. It's less fun to actually live through working for leaders like Priestly regardless of their gender. The good news is that Gallup organization found that the majority, 52 percent, of German workers say a leader's gender does not matter to them at all. In the same study, they also found among the remaining workers who do have a preference, a whopping 34 percent would prefer working for a man.

The image of the overly aggressive woman leader concerned only with results to the detriment of the people around her may be a misperception of women leaders that many people have. A study about the differences between women and men as leaders at Harvard Business School found the style differences between women and men as leaders to be very small.

One difference they found, contrary to our image of Priestly, is that most women leaders are more democratic and participative than men. Men are much more likely to assume a command and control, directive leadership style. The researchers also reported that it is not always good to be a participative leader. There is a middle ground somewhere in between being too democratic and being highly authoritative that effective leaders of all genders must find.

Women who achieve success in the senior executive ranks of leadership are able to find and maintain this balanced style—concerned both with the people in the organization and the business results. When Judi Johansen was appointed as the president of Marylhurst University, after having served as president and CEO of PacifiCorp, the announcement from the board said, "She is a proven organizational leader and strategic thinker. She is a good listener and quick learner. She knows how to bring out the best in people, including those with expertise beyond her own. She is a relationship builder. She has financial acumen." Johansen is a great example of a woman leader who is able to balance the needs of people with the need to achieve business results. Johansen rose to a C Suite position in a highly male-dominated utility industry and was highly respected as a leader by both women and men. Very few of us have the experience of working for women like Johansen.

Anne Mulcahy, the former CEO of Xerox, is another example of finding this middle ground. Mulcahy revealed that she had to learn to embrace power and learn effective decision making. In an article in *Fortune*, she said, "I used to define power as influence—that you gotta get everyone's vote. So it doesn't feel like power. It feels like consensus. But I've learned that a decision needs to be made. A call needs to be made." Mulcahy's rise to the chief executive officer position is often referred to as an accident, surprise, or unplanned event, even by her. Her appointment to the position was criticized at the time by people like Jack Welch, former CEO of General Electric. Welch viewed the appointment of a woman to the highest level leadership position in a company that was in need of a financial and cultural turnaround as tempting fate. Mulcahy learned the position and was responsible for saving Xerox from imminent bankruptcy.

Despite the examples set by women like Johansen and Mulcahy, men are still more likely to emerge as leaders, according to a study at the University of Buffalo. The researchers attribute the gap of women in leadership positions to societal norms and personality differences. Men are expected to be more assertive and dominant. Those are characteristics that people associate with effective leadership. Characteristics like sensitivity and showing concern for others made someone less likely to be perceived as a leader. The researchers say it's no surprise with these perceptions that women hold only about 26 percent of executive level positions in the S&P 500 company list.

Our perceptions about personality differences between women and men may be more than stereotype or bias. The Myers Briggs Type Indicator (MBTI) is one of the most commonly used personality assessments across the globe. It has been translated into 26 languages, validated and updated for over 40 years. The one gender difference that remains constant is a difference between women and men in the approach to decision making. The majority of women, approximately 60 percent, use the feeling preference when making decisions. When making a decision, people who prefer the feeling preference consider first information like the alignment of a decision with values and the impact on people affected by the outcome.

People who prefer the feeling preference are also less likely to score well on assessments that measure critical thinking approaches such as evaluating arguments and drawing conclusions. The majority of men prefer the thinking approach to decision making. People who prefer the thinking preference rely first on approaches like logical analysis when asked to make a decision. Neither preference is better than the other. Each preference has its strengths. There are many examples of poor business decisions made that were entirely logical.

The Ford Pinto tragedy is one example. In this historic case, a decision was made to keep the Pinto on the market when it was discovered that the car featured a gas tank that would explode when struck from the rear. The decision makers considered a cost-benefit analysis as the primary reason. After several deaths, Ford faced controversy and lawsuits. This decision making blunder helps illustrate the need for both approaches in everyday decisions and in the corporate boardroom. The most effective decisions are made when we consider the impact on people—customers, suppliers, and employees. We must also consider the financial cost, the logic, and plan appropriately for implementation. Our views of effective leadership must change to incorporate both approaches to decision making.

According to the American Association of University Women (AAUW), the gap of women in leadership positions is even more striking in the United States when we look at the number of women represented in elected political positions. Women make up only 19 percent of elected officials. The gap of women in leadership persists in business, universities, courts, and nonprofit religious institutions. AAUW also points out that this gap is bad for business. Companies with women in executive leadership positions have higher performance and profits.

Pew Research Center says that while many women and men agree there are too few women in leadership positions, a primary reason that we have fewer women in the roles is that women have to do more to prove they can handle the position. Pew researchers also found that women are more likely to encounter structural barriers, uneven expectations, and discrimination. The results show that the majority of both women and men say that men have an easier path to get to the top leadership positions in business and politics.

Anne Cummings, a former professor at Wharton, says that our perceptions of leadership as a position are largely masculine. Many of the qualities we view as the characteristics of an effective leader, we associate with male traits. Cummings led seminars filled with executive women during which she often asked them to brainstorm words describing women leaders and men leaders. The differences she found were that the words used to describe men as leaders were often words such as powerful, intelligent, assertive, and direct. Words used to describe women as leaders were emotional, empathetic, relationship oriented, and gossipy. Our perceptions about the effectiveness of women as leaders can be just as important to our performance as the actual ability of women leaders.

Only when we shift our thinking about the qualities we associate with effective leadership will women be viewed as leaders able to inspire people, make quality decisions, and lead teams to achieve exceptional business performance.

Success Strategies

There are three strategies for overcoming this myth. First, you must create your own vision of what effective leadership is. Second, sharpen your decision-making skills by practicing a variety of methods and approaches.

Third, take every opportunity to develop leadership skills rather than learning by trial and error after you are in the formal role.

Vision of Leadership

It would be nice if everyone in the world would begin to shift perceptions of what effective leadership is, what they do, and how they behave. Recognizing that in reality there are perceptions that exist and define leadership as primarily masculine, we can start with ourselves. Before stepping into a leadership position, you can think about your own perceptions, your vision of leadership, and the type of leader you will be. Experienced leaders also find it helpful to consider a vision of leadership, how they are perceived by others, and changes they can make. It's especially helpful to share your vision of leadership with others when you accept a new position, add new direct reports to an existing team, or make changes within an organization.

Some of the key areas to consider as you define a vision of leadership include your values and your personal leadership style. Researchers have found that to be perceived as successful leaders, women must be able to appear both traditionally feminine—affectionate, kind, caring, and nurturing—and traditionally masculine—ambitious, independent, assertive, and forceful. It's a paradox and a double bind that does not apply to men. Men may be perceived as effective leaders without demonstrating the traditionally feminine qualities.

Think about what is most important to you as a leader of other people. You must give thought to how you will manage the tension between behaviors that may be viewed as polar opposites like being perceived as caring and forceful when leading others. There may be some issues within an organization that you are willing to fight for and others that you would consider trivial. Your expectations about how people on your team will support each other, work together, or work independently toward a common goal must be clarified for the people who report to you. There may be behavior that you have witnessed on a team that you were a part of that you will not tolerate as a leader.

It's also important to realize when you are promoted to a leadership role for the first time your approach toward work must change from a focus on getting the work done to creating shared common goals and guiding others to achieve. Each time you advance to a higher level of leadership, you must think about the requirements for the new role and how the leadership role is different, and create a vision of your leadership approach.

According to one study reported in *Chief Learning Officer* magazine, only 11 percent of people that transition into a leadership role from an individual contributor position are actually coached or groomed in advance for the position. The shift to leadership is frustrating, challenging, and stressful for 87 percent of people. McKinsey & Company report that transitions from mid-level to executive leadership are equally as difficult with a 40 to 50 percent rate of failure. Without a clear vision of your leadership approach and thought given to how you will shift your behavior, the odds for success are simply not in your favor. As more women are able to successfully navigate the transition into leadership roles at all levels, others perceptions of leadership may change. We will see more examples of great women leaders who bring the best of both the stereotypically masculine and feminine traits to effective leadership.

Sharpen Decision-Making Skills

All leaders regardless of gender can benefit from honing the ability to make decisions. For women, it may be especially important to focus on this area understanding that often women prefer to use a more participative approach, consider values, and the impact of a decision on other people. There are numerous books and training courses available about different methods of decision making, ranging from full inclusion of others to the authoritarian approach.

It's always important to consider the urgency of the issue and the level of involvement you really need from others. Adjust the efforts you make to include others in a decision based upon the situation. Involving others has great benefits like the diversity of perspectives. It also takes more time to reach agreement. This requires self-awareness, flexibility, and thought given to each decision rather than relying upon one approach that has worked for you in the past.

It's important to consider your personality style when it comes to the way you approach decision making. There are many different personality assessments, but one that may be helpful in improving our approach to decisions is the MBTI. The MBTI assessment is based upon the theories

of Carl Jung, a Swiss psychologist. It identifies four personality preferences that when combined, make up our four letter personality type. Two
of the preferences are especially important to decision making.

According to the theory, one preference that each person has is related
to how he or she gathers information—either by sensing or by intuition.
People who prefer sensing tend to focus more on the detail, the literal information, and the facts. People who prefer intuition as a preference tend
to focus more on the big picture, generating alternatives and imaginative
new ideas. In any decision-making scenario, we can benefit from using
both these preferences. When you are self aware and understand your
typical approach or strength, you can adapt your method to gathering
information about the decision to be made by also using your opposite
preference, whether it is sensing or intuition.

The other MBTI preference that explains differences in our approach
to decision making is the preference for thinking or feeling. Both the
thinking preference, relying on the practical logic, and the feeling preference, aligning with values and the human impact of the decision, are
equally valuable. We can apply the knowledge about MBTI preferences
to make the highest quality decisions if we can use all four of these preferences: sensing, intuition, thinking, and feeling when we make decisions.
Consider the information, the vision, the logic, and the impact on people
any time you approach a decision.

Develop Leadership Skills Before Gaining the Job Title

Becoming a great leader by trial and error can be painful and unforgiving. Company cultures are different in their tolerance level for mistakes.
One organization may provide a wealth of leadership training and formal
coaching or mentoring when someone is promoted into a formal leadership
role. Many other organizations will have no training, coaching, or mentoring for new leaders stepping into a management position for the first time.
Regardless of the company culture, if you aspire to a leadership position, it
is important to find opportunities yourself to practice and develop skills.
Leadership is about influencing others, often without a formal job title. One
of the best ways to gain experience without the risk of an unforgiving company culture is to volunteer for leadership positions outside the company.

There are many nonprofit organizations, community groups, and professional associations seeking people to fill leadership positions. The skills you can learn include managing a budget, directing a project, marketing, communications, facilitating effective meetings, fundraising, and inspiring others to perform. Motivating volunteers to accomplish work when they don't have any financial incentives to complete the assignments may even be a more difficult environment to practice leading others. Select a cause that interests you, set a goal for improving your leadership skills, and contribute to the community.

It's equally important to raise your voice and volunteer to lead new projects and teams within your company. Women face the challenge of being overlooked for leadership positions. Make certain others in the organization know about your career aspirations, look for people who are willing to support them, and ask for the opportunity to lead.

Assess Yourself and Plan for Development

This purpose of self-assessment is to help you enhance your effectiveness. This tool can help you chart your progress over time. It can also help you discover your strengths and development areas. Use the information to guide discussions with your manager and others in your network who can support your career development. You may also use the questions to solicit feedback from others.

Assess Yourself

Instructions: Read each question item and rate yourself on a scale of 1 to 5.

- 1 = I need serious improvement in this area.
- 2 = I need some improvement in this area.
- 3 = I'm talented and skilled in this area.
- 4 = A strength for me.
- 5 = A major strength. I consider myself a role model for other women.

Chapter 9 Assessment	Rating				
1. I have a clear vision of my leadership style and approach to leading others.	1	2	3	4	5
2. I am aware of my preferred approach to decision making, whether it is logical and systematic, or one centered on values and the impact on people.	1	2	3	4	5
3. I am aware of how I gather information when I need to decide, whether I prefer detailed information or a broad vision.	1	2	3	4	5
4. I am skilled in using a variety of decision-making methods ranging from full involvement and consensus to announcing my decision to others with little or no input.	1	2	3	4	5
5. I communicate with others about my vision of leadership and what is important to know about working for me.	1	2	3	4	5
6. I am effectively balancing my leadership style between both the positive aspects of both stereotypically masculine and feminine traits.	1	2	3	4	5
7. I have informed others about my career aspirations and desire to hold a leadership position.	1	2	3	4	5
8. I have taken action to learn leadership skills by volunteering to lead teams or projects inside or outside my company.	1	2	3	4	5
9. I have considered how the leadership position that I aspire to or occupy now is different from my past role and created a plan for my transition into that role.	1	2	3	4	5
10. I watch for role models and learn from the methods that successful women leaders use to navigate barriers in the workplace.	1	2	3	4	5
Calculate Your Overall Average Rating					

Plan for Development

Reflect on your assessment score and plan for your future. If your overall average rating is a 4 or 5, personal presence and communication style is a strength for you. If your average rating is a 1, 2, or 3, presence and communication style could become a career derailer. On the question items where you rated yourself a 4 or 5, consider new ways to leverage your strengths. If you rated yourself a 1, 2, or 3, consider the implications for your career. These areas could get in the way of your future success. Use the ideas for leveraging strengths and developing opportunity areas to create a plan for career development.

Leverage strengths

- Interview other women you admire or read about them to learn lessons about leadership.
- Share your own vision and view about leadership with a group of other people. Be transparent about your accomplishments, as well as mistakes you have made in your career and what you learned from them.
- Increase your comfort level with high-risk decisions. Practice evaluating alternatives in risky situations and coming to conclusions quickly.
- Model effective decision-making techniques by leading a meeting where you demonstrate an approach to reaching agreement.
- Provide opportunities for other women to colead a project and learn from you.

Develop opportunities

- Reflect upon your leadership vision. Write a description of your leadership style, guiding values, and your approach to leading others. Share it with others, so they won't have to guess about what is most important to you.
- Think carefully about your current or future leadership position. Define the requirements of the current position and how you must change your past approach to be successful in the new role.
- Ask for feedback from others on their perception of your leadership style and behaviors that help or hinder others from performing. Then take action to balance your approach with a combination of the best traditionally masculine or feminine leadership qualities.
- Complete an assessment or reflect on your approach to decision making. Then, adapt your approach to fit the situation. Research and apply a new tool for critical thinking or method that incorporates all personality preferences for gathering information and deciding.
- Ask direct reports, key stakeholders, and customers for input in making decisions when you must have long-term support and co-operation. In situations where decisions have stalled for too long, move people forward by informing others of your decision.

- Gain leadership experience by volunteering to lead others either through an organization outside of work or a new assignment in your current role.

Additional Resources

Bonney, G. 2016. *In the Company of Women: Inspiration and Advice from Over 100 Makers, Artists and Entrepreneurs.* New York, NY: Artisan Books.

Charan, R., S. Drotter, and J. Noel. 2011 *The Leadership Pipeline: How to Build a Leadership Powered Company.* San Francisco, CA: Jossey-Bass.

Hegelsen, S., and M. Goldsmith. 2018. *How Women Rise: Break the 12 Habits Holding You Back from Your Next Raise, Promotion, or Job.* New York, NY: Hachette Books.

Ibarra, H., D. Tannen, J. Williams, and S.A. Hewlett . 2018. *HBR's 10 Must Reads on Women and Leadership.* Boston, MA: Harvard Business Review.

Myers Briggs Type Indicator. "People Development Solutions Used by 88 of the Fortune 100 Companies," *The Myers Briggs Company.* https://www.themyersbriggs.com

Watkins, M. 2013. *The First 90 Days: Proven Strategies for Getting Up to Speed Faster and Smarter, Updated and Expanded.* Boston, MA: Harvard Business Publishing.

CHAPTER 10

Myth: When Women Report Inappropriate Behavior Such as Harassment or Bullying, the Behavior Will Stop

I have learned over the years that when one's mind is made up, this diminishes fear; knowing what must be done does away with fear.

—Rosa Parks

He was a very tall, strong, muscular man. When they met to discuss progress on work projects assigned to her, his body towered over her petite frame. They had never disagreed on how to approach any situation. One day without warning, he looked into her eyes, grabbed her by the shoulders, shook her violently, and screamed his opinion at her. He then lifted her by her shoulders out of her chair and swung her body across the room. As he lifted her above his head, he placed the collar of her jacket over the coat rack on the back of her office door. He left her there. She was hanging by the coat rack on the back of her office door. This story may seem a little far-fetched—hanging on an office door coat rack.

It isn't. It happened to a woman. There are millions of other seemingly far-fetched stories that we learn only from the stories of other women when we talk about them. Another woman left her profession because her manager kept touching her inappropriately. She was unable to find another position in her field. Two women with completely different professional career paths talking at a cocktail party were encouraged to exchange bully stories. A third woman who made the introduction shared that the two of them had a common experience. After talking, they discovered that the experience of being the target of inappropriate behavior was not the only thing they had in common. They both were actually targeted by the same man.

There is no shame in being harassed or bullied by someone. Sally Kane wrote a career article identifying many reasons a person is chosen. It may boil down to the harasser or bully feeling insecure, jealous, and wanting control over the person. In competitive corporate environments, high-performing women are often on the receiving end of harmful, aggressive, and mean-spirited behavior. The aggressor may be a man or another woman. According to the Workplace Bullying Institute, women are 60 percent of the people targeted. The U.S. Equal Employment Opportunity Commission (EEOC) statistics on sexual harassment charges files show that approximately 83 percent of the charges are filed by women.

Almost every human resources training program on the subject of harassment instructs the recipient of unwelcome physical or sexual behavior to tell the other person to stop in the moment. Intellectually, it sounds as though every woman who attends the training would be ready and prepared to confront the situation. Emotionally, it does not prepare women to respond in the moment of shock, surprise, and fear if the perpetrator is the boss with control over future performance ratings, compensation, and assignments. Research conducted by the Workplace Bullying Institute says that 71 percent of companies react to cases of reported abusive behavior in ways that actually harm the targeted person.

Most human resources professionals want to create a safe, healthy, and productive workplace for all employees. The people who work in human resources, though, must operate in the same company environment where the unwanted behavior occurred. According to studies conducted by affiliates of the Society for Human Resources Management, about 60 percent of professionals who work in the human resources department experience bullying, intimidation, and an offensive work environment too. Investigations of inappropriate conduct are conducted but without solid evidence, documentation, or witnesses who are willing to speak up, there is often limited action that can be taken.

Often in a case with conflicting testimonies by the two parties involved, the immediate outcome is an interrogation of the accused person. Legal harassment, discrimination, and even physical assault can be difficult to prove. An angry, abusive jerk with power over your future performance ratings, work assignments, career opportunities, or work hours does not typically make the work situation easier to navigate.

Favoritism in the form of giving one employee preferred work assignments over another employee regardless of their gender is not illegal. Failing to share information, leaving an employee out of a critical meeting, speaking harshly about someone in front of coworkers, and providing constant negative feedback is poor management technique. Investigators may argue that it isn't legally discrimination because many people have seen the person harass both men and women.

Harassers and bullies seem to have become more savvy about laws and creative in recent years. A team of researchers in the UK found that cyberbullying and cyberstalking using social media, the Internet, and a variety of electronic tools has a traumatic impact on the victim. While the majority of people will experience some type of bullying in their lifetimes, they say there is much more work to be done in identifying ways to respond and to eliminate this behavior legally. This may sound like bleak news.

There are a few companies that have found healthy and effective ways to live the values that are posted on the office walls, eliminate offensive behavior, combat harassers, screen out bullies, and develop effective leaders. Professor Robert Sutton at Stanford University wrote about many of them years ago in a book titled *The No Asshole Rule*. These companies recognize that bad behavior has a negative financial impact on the company and a damaging emotional impact on people. One company that Sutton wrote about found ways to quantify the financial impact of poor leadership behavior and held the individual accountable.

Not all companies are this effective, and some even intentionally hire aggressive leaders in the interest of obtaining immediate, often short-term, results. Sutton said one of his primary reasons for writing the book is that his research showed that mean behavior is contagious. The person on the receiving end of bad behavior that is left unaddressed is at risk of lowering his or her standards personally to become an asshole, bully, or harasser. A company culture is formed with a ripple effect of each person's behavior.

Change has never been easy for women. Hardships haven't always been discussed openly. In the United States, a few years ago high school textbooks often had a short paragraph or two about the women's suffrage movement. It most likely included little detail, no information about violence, no hunger strikes, or even recognition of the women activists who fought for the passage of the 19th Amendment. A review of textbooks at Minnesota State University revealed that the opportunity to describe the injustices on women so that we could learn from them has been completely missed by the authors teaching our children.

The #MeToo movement has raised awareness in recent years. We have seen more women march in awareness parades than at any time in the past five decades. Women have come forward to support other women who raise concerns, even when they personally have had nothing to gain from it. The American Bar Association cautions companies against closing complaints just because they are no longer legally actionable according to the legal requirements for filing a legal claim. They acknowledge that in the past some companies had kept the secrets of senior-level executives seen as too high on the organization chart to fall. An organization may be found liable for ignoring inappropriate behavior of powerful people. This is progress.

Success Strategies

There are five strategies for overcoming this myth. First, always prioritize your personal safety, health, and wellness. Second, speak up in the situation and tell the other person to stop. Third, document the facts. Fourth, cautiously assess the risk of reporting the behavior. Then, carefully plan your escape route for leaving the situation.

Safety, Health, and Wellness Is Priority #1

Safety always comes first. In the end, it will not matter if there are any witnesses or evidence. It doesn't matter if anyone in the world believes what you say happened in your situation. Your best friend may think you are exaggerating. Others in your office or career network may know and like the person who has bullied and physically assaulted you. The only thing that will actually make a difference to you is that you come home from work safe each day. Your personal safety includes both your physical and mental health and wellness.

Many years ago, a woman accepted a position that appeared to be a good career opportunity. It was with a well-known company. She thought that having this position, experience, and company brand on her resume was exactly what she needed to propel her career forward. She underestimated the impact of accepting a position that reported to a bully. She spent her lunch hour each day walking to the parking lot, climbing into her car, closing the door, and crying in a place where no one else could see her. She thought if she could last a year in the position, then she would be prepared to interview, explain what she learned, and be ready for the next position. The emotional impact of working in an unhealthy, toxic environment can be devastating to a career and deadly.

The National Institutes of Health research confirms that stress can have a direct impact on physical health. Depending on the severity and duration of the stress, some of the areas that can be affected include the ability to learn, decision making, memory of information, and the functioning of your heart. People under severe and prolonged stress may also weaken their immune system. This means they will be more likely to experience disease and sickness. This clearly isn't good for any business. Increased absenteeism and the higher cost of health care has a negative impact on company profits. Skipping work to take a mental health day to rest or get outdoors is a common phenomenon in unhealthy work environments. More importantly, the effects of enduring extreme stress over time may have a negative impact on your performance and career.

Basic self-defense knowledge and techniques are important in the event of a serious physical assault. There are a wealth of experts and resources for women that teach how to respond to a physical threat. Techniques often include increasing your awareness, demonstrating vocal confidence, and responding to physical threat.

Tell the Person to Stop

This advice has been consistent for many years in the legal and human resources professions. There are legal reasons why you should let the other person know that the behavior is unwelcome. This book is not intended to be a legal training or reference. There are other reasons you must speak up. You must tell the other person that you are offended because if they don't realize the impact of their behavior, they will not have the opportunity to change. If you have offended someone at work, you would want to be given the benefit of the doubt and the opportunity to make amends. Communicate to the person in a calm, precise way. Start by explaining in a factual way exactly what they did. Facts are observable and hard to argue with. When you state the facts about what occurred, you are less likely to receive a defensive or emotional reaction from the other person. Then tell the other person why it was offensive to you. Explain the impact the behavior had and clearly ask him or her to stop.

Even if the other person has no intention of changing his evil ways, the act of telling him to stop is powerful. You will never be able to control the other person's behavior or his response to you. You only have control over what you say to the other person in this uncomfortable situation and what you will do when someone offends, harasses, or bullies you. It takes courage and confidence to speak calmly. Express the facts, why it is important, and tell him to stop the unwanted behavior. It is the only way to feel empowered in the situation.

Document the Facts

Always document the inappropriate behavior and your response. Keep a clear legible record of the date, time, witnesses if any, and specifically what was said and done by each person present. If the behavior continues and escalates in severity, if you choose to report the behavior you will need the information. If there are written examples of the behavior and your response in the form of e-mails, text messages, or other communications, keep this information as well. There isn't much more to say about this, except that it is critical as evidence that the behavior occurred. Don't rely on your memory to remember every detail. Enough said. Write it down.

Assess the Risk of Reporting the Behavior

In an ideal world, everyone would report the behavior to an authority. Evidence of wrongdoing would be found, and the aggressor would be stopped. Witnesses would intervene or speak up to support the person receiving the unwanted behavior. We aren't living in an ideal world yet. This means that you must know that when you report the behavior, your situation may or may not improve. Think carefully about the situation and assess the risk of reporting the behavior.

Consider what you know about the aggressor. Important factors might include his or her length of tenure within the company, reputation, relationships with others in the company, the level of power he or she holds, and any factual information you have about a history of previous complaints. Consider what you know about yourself. Important factors to consider might include your length of time with the company, your relationships with others in the company, your desire to continue working there, and your need for a positive career reference.

In the world we live in today, you won't always be able to rely on others, including witnesses or other people who have been attacked by the same person, to support you. One woman who had experienced harassment told another woman targeted by the same person, "I want to continue working here. I am sorry, but I won't speak up for you. This bully has damaged my career enough already. Others have tried to report the behavior, everyone knows about it, and nothing is ever done." When everyone takes responsibility and feels empowered to speak up against behavior that is clearly wrong, the world may change. Today, it is important to think carefully about the best and worst thing that could happen to you personally after you report the behavior. Weigh the pros and cons. Then choose to take the action that is best for you.

Plan Your Escape Route

In many scenarios, the aggressive persons are unwilling to change their behavior. In other situations they may be able to change. There are executive coaches who specialize in helping leaders better manage emotions and change their approach toward employees. This type of behavior change from threatening to empowering others takes time. Even when you use superior communication skills and manage the other person well, when the timing is right for your career, often the best outcome is leaving the situation. It can be extremely disappointing to go into a new position with excitement and the expectation that it will be a good learning opportunity. Sometimes the most you will learn will be how to feel confident and empowered in the presence of a tyrant.

One woman found herself in a toxic situation working for a downright mean manager. She chose to leave the position after a month. She didn't mince words with the manager who treated her poorly. She was direct and honest about her reason for leaving. She also chose not to include the position on her resume or offer that manager's name as a reference during interviews for her next position. She was concerned about getting a bad reference from the manager. There was a risk in not revealing this information. Her future employer could have found out in a small town or small network of people in her profession in a large city. The next company could have viewed her omission of this information as dishonest. For her, it was a risk worth taking. She was established enough in her career to have other people to provide positive references. She found another position very quickly and never suffered any negative consequences.

Another woman with a similar experience took the risk of leaving the job immediately. She then openly explained to interviewers for her next position that she was unable to work for the manager in her previous position. She carefully described some of the specific factual behaviors she had experienced working for the person. The risk in revealing this information during the interview for the next position is that the interviewers have the power to interpret it and make a decision. They will attempt to understand the information shared with them about the situation in a short time frame without all of the evidence. They will consider the skills and experience she holds. They will also think about the culture within the company and decide if she is capable of communicating and working with the management in the new position. In this situation, the interviewers appreciated her honesty. They believed that their company culture and management approach was different than the situation shared with them. The woman was offered the new job.

There isn't one best escape route that works for everyone. You must think about the current situation. As you consider the situation, think about the severity and impact of the behavior and the time frame you can endure it, whether it is one more day or one more year. It's up to you to also think about your future. Your future includes the specific type of position you want to be in next, how you will transition from where you are now, and a plan on the specific actions you will take to get there.

Assess Yourself and Plan for Development

This purpose of self-assessment is to help you enhance your effectiveness. This tool can help you chart your progress over time. It can also help you discover your strengths and development areas. Use the information to guide discussions with your manager and others in your network who can support your career development. You may also use the questions to solicit feedback from others.

Assess Yourself

Instructions: Read each question item and rate yourself on a scale of 1 to 5.

- 1 = I need serious improvement in this area.
- 2 = I need some improvement in this area.
- 3 = I'm talented and skilled in this area.
- 4 = A strength for me.
- 5 = A major strength. I consider myself a role model for other women.

Chapter 10 Assessment	Rating				
1. My personal safety, health, and wellness is a top priority, even if it means leaving my current job.	1	2	3	4	5
2. I am confident and able to tell another person that his or her behavior is offensive or unwelcome and that I want it to stop.	1	2	3	4	5
3. I am able to remain calm, communicate factual information and the impact of another person's behavior.	1	2	3	4	5
4. I document inappropriate behavior when it occurs in the workplace whether it is directed at me or another person.	1	2	3	4	5
5. I can assess the risk associated in reporting inappropriate behavior and take action that minimizes the negative impact on me.	1	2	3	4	5
6. I plan ahead and think clearly about how I will leave a toxic or unhealthy work situation if needed.	1	2	3	4	5
7. When I witness inappropriate behavior in the workplace, I am willing to speak up, intervene, and help others at the risk of becoming a target myself.	1	2	3	4	5
8. I recognize the physical warning signs when stress is having a negative impact on my health and emotional well-being.	1	2	3	4	5
9. Before I accept a new position, I ask about and observe the manager's style and the company culture to assess how I may be treated.	1	2	3	4	5
10. I know how to use some basic self-defense techniques for protecting myself against a physical assault.	1	2	3	4	5
Calculate Your Overall Average Rating					

Plan for Development

Reflect on your assessment score and plan for your future. If your overall average rating is a 4 or 5, personal presence and communication style is a strength for you. If your average rating is a 1, 2, or 3, presence and communication style could become a career derailer. On the question items where you rated yourself a 4 or 5, consider new ways to leverage your strengths. If you rated yourself a 1, 2, or 3, consider the implications for your career. These areas could get in the way of your future success. Use the ideas for leveraging strengths and developing opportunity areas to create a plan for career development.

Leverage strengths
- Hold a discussion with others about the code of conduct, values, or acceptable behavior in the workplace.
- Assess the culture in your work environment and look for signs that unacceptable behavior is being addressed appropriately. Identify ways to improve accountability.
- Volunteer to lead a committee responsible for improving the safety and health of people at work. Discuss ways you might be able to prevent threatening situations and encourage safe reporting methods.
- Identify specific times at work where offensive behavior may occur such as a meeting where you anticipate conflict. Take action to discuss ground rules for behavior and set expectations for how you will interact before the discussion begins.
- Help others set boundaries and intervene when you see someone make an offensive comment toward someone else or behave in a manner that appears to be unwelcome or inappropriate for the workplace.

Develop opportunities
- Practice delivering a message about offensive behavior in an open and direct manner. Role play asking a person to stop a behavior with a trusted partner who will respond in an angry, threatening, or emotional tone. Ask for feedback about how you could improve.

- Avoid working for a bully by developing a list of interview questions that you will use to assess whether or not a manager is someone you can work for. Screen them out before you accept a career opportunity.
- Develop a list of questions to assess a company's culture during the interview process. Have a thorough understanding of the work environment and the job. Research company reviews on sites such as Glassdoor.com. Look for comments about culture and tolerance for bullies and offensive behavior.
- Find support by connecting with organizations dedicated to the prevention of harassment and bullying in the workplace.
- Create a plan for monitoring your health and well-being. Activities might include a new exercise routine, a healthier diet, or monitoring your work hours.
- Learn some basic self-defense techniques for protecting yourself against a physical assault.

Additional Resources

Borysenko, K. September, 2018. *Zen Your Work: Create Your Ideal Work Experience Through Mindful Self-Mastery.* New York, NY: TarcherPerigee.

Crawshaw, L. 2007. *Taming the Abrasive Manager at Work: How to End Unnecessary Roughness in the Workplace.* San Francisco, CA, US: Jossey-Bass.

Garnier, K. 2004. Movie *Iron Jawed Angels* www.imbd.com/title/tt0338139

Lechtenberg, B. "Safety Courses for Adults and Seniors." http://www.brettlechtenberg.com/adults-seniors

Namie, G. (November, 2009). *The Bully at Work: What You Can Do to Stop the Hurt and Reclaim Your Dignity on the Job.* Naperville, IL: SourceBooks Inc.

Sutton, R. (September, 2010). *The No Asshole Rule: Building a Civilized Workplace and Surviving One That Isn't.* New York, NY: Business Plus.

CHAPTER 11

Putting It All Together in a Development Plan

I always wondered why somebody doesn't do something about that.
Then I realized I was somebody.

—Lily Tomlin

This book explores career myths and the true barriers that women may encounter at work. It has offered you the opportunity to assess yourself, reflect on your strengths, and development areas at the end of each chapter. True change only comes with action. Use the three steps below to identify one or two areas for focused action. Then, create a plan for moving forward to overcome the myths and achieve greater satisfaction and success in your career.

Development Plan

Step 1: Review your self-assessment ratings at the end of each chapter. Use the chart below to record your overall average rating for each chapter. Place a check mark by the highest and lowest rated chapters.

Chapter	Overall Average Rating	Highest Rated	Lowest Rated
1			
2			
3			
4			
5			
6			
7			
8			
9			
10			

Step 2: Use the space provided to identify one or two areas of focus. These should be areas that you are motivated to take action and achieve real progress. You may want to reflect on the specific question items on the self-assessment at the end of the chapter. Choose one or two strengths to leverage or one or two areas for development.

Focus Area 1:
Focus Area 2:

Step 3: Create a specific plan for moving forward to enhance your effectiveness at work. You may want to use the information to guide discussions with your manager and others in your network who can support your career development. There are additional development resources such as books and videos included in this book at the end of each chapter.

Focus Area	Activity/ Action	Priority High Medium Low	Status In Progress Complete Not Started	Start Date	Complete Date

CHAPTER 12

Moving Beyond the Myth

You cannot hope to build a better world without improving the individuals. To that end, each of us must work for his own improvement and, at the same time, share a general responsibility for all humanity, our particular duty being to aid those to whom we think we can be most useful.

—Marie Curie

This book is written with the input of many women about myths or self-limiting beliefs that can have a detrimental impact on their career success. The stories shared and success strategies come directly from the real life experiences of women. Some of the advice comes from things they wish they had known earlier in their careers. Other tips are based on the actions they used to overcome real career barriers in the workplace. The intent of the book is to help women advance and to achieve their full potential. That does not mean the book is written only for women to read.

Both women and men must be aware of the barriers women face in the workplace. Women must be able to talk openly about the challenges, learn from the experience of other women, take responsibility for their careers, and identify specific actions for their own career development. An individual woman can read this book, identify strengths, recognize development areas, and create an action plan.

Women must also be able to learn from men. Men have shared stories and real life examples about women they have hired or coached, who later advanced to executive level positions. Those women may not have been as successful without that support. The majority of senior executive level positions in corporations are still occupied by men. Men play a critical role in helping women rise to that level.

Men have also expressed interest in learning more about what they can do to encourage the advancement of talented women they know. After a recent educational session, one of the few men present said that he wished men would fill half the seats in the room. He was there to learn, share his perspectives about career, and to take action to help women. The most important ingredient in career mentorship and coaching is finding people in your network that you admire and trust.

A young professional woman who had never experienced any of the barriers in this book was startled early in her career when a man told her that one day she would probably be bullied or harassed. He had hired her, promoted her, given her challenging assignments, and listened to her recommendations on the job. There was no question about his intent. He was to prepare her for something that eventually would happen many years later. Women need to find both men and women to look up to as effective role models and to trust to offer career advice, ongoing feedback, and coaching.

True knowledge, ah ha moments, and creative ideas come from sharing diverse perspectives in any field of work. The same is true when it comes to learning about how to advance a career in the workplace. Women and men must have open dialogue about the potential hurdles women may face during their careers and how to overcome them. We all share the responsibility for helping women across the globe rise to higher levels and achieve their full potential.

CHAPTER 13

Bibliography

Follow your instincts, that's where true wisdom will manifest.

—Oprah Winfrey

Chapter 2

Adewunmi, B. 2014. "Male Presenter Wears Same Suit for a Year Does Anyone Notice?" https://www.theguardian.com/lifeandstyle/womens-blog/2014/nov/17/male-tv-presenter-same-suit-year-female-colleagues-judged

Dishman, L. 2016. "New G-mail Plug In Highlights Words and Phrases that Undermine Your Message." https://www.fastcompany.com/3055071/new-gmail-plug-in-highlights-words-and-phrases-that-undermine-your-message

Judge, T. 2004. "The Effect of Physical Height on Workplace Success and Income: Preliminary Test of a Theoretical Model." *Journal of Applied Psychology* 89, no. 3, pp. 428–41. http://timothy-judge.com/Height%20paper--JAP%20published.pdf

Lallo, M. 2014. "Karl Stefanovic's Sexism Experiment: Today Presenter Wears Same Suit for a Year." https://www.smh.com.au/entertainment/tv-and-radio/karl-stefanovics-sexism-experiment-today-presenter-wears-same-suit-for-a-year-20141115-11ncdz.html#ixzz3JL2gKTRM

Lebowitz, S. 2015. "Science Says Being Tall Could Make You Richer and More Successful—Here's Why." http://www.businessinsider.com/tall-people-are-richer-and-successful-2015-9

Mehrabian, A. 1972. *Silent Messages: Implicit Communication of Emotions and Attitudes.* Belmont, CA: Wadsworth Publishing Co Inc.

Molloy, J. 1996. *New Women's Dress for Success.* New York, NY: Warner Books.

Molloy, J. 1977. *Women's Dress for Success.* New York, NY: Warner Books.

Mohindra, V., and S. Azhar. 2012. "Gender Communication: A Comparative Analysis of Communicational Approaches of Men and Women at Workplaces." http://www.iosrjournals.org/iosr-jhss/papers/Vol2-issue1/D0211827.pdf

Parker, K., J. Horowitz, and R. Stepler. 2017. "On Gender Differences, No Consensus on Nature vs. Nurture," *Pew Research.* http://www.pewsocialtrends.org/2017/12/05/on-gender-differences-no-consensus-on-nature-vs-nurture

Wilkes, D. 2016. "It's Not Just the Economy Pluging in the Red: Theresa May Makes the Most of it Too, Stealing the 2016 Budget Show with a Dress Which Divides Twitter." http://www.dailymail.co.uk/news/article-3495666/Put-yer-baps-away-darling-Theresa-steals-budget-dress-divides-Twitter.html

Wilson, C. 2017. "The Royal Family's Dress Code Uncovered." http://www.bbc.com/news/uk-40640634

Chapter 3

De Pater, I., A. E. M. Van Vianen, and M. N. Bechtoldt. 2010. "Tilburg University Gender Differences in Job Challenge A Matter of Task Allocation," https://www.tilburguniversity.edu/upload/e49c2b37-b321-431b-8bcaa93ded3dd85d_onderzoek%20%20gender%20differences%20in%20job%20challange.pdf

Guadagno, R. E., and R. B. Cialdini. 2007. "Gender Differences in Impression Management in Organizations: A Qualitative Review." http://citeseerx.ist.psu.edu/viewdoc/download?doi=10.1.1.492.6656&rep=rep1&type=pdf

Hansen, F. 2017. "Entrepreneur Corporate Politics and Toxic Environments are the Real Reasons Women are 'Learning Out.'" https://www.entrepreneur.com/amphtml/297165

Karson, M. 2017. "Why Do People Hate Smart Women?" *Psychology Today,* https://www.psychologytoday.com/us/blog/feeling-our-way/201711/why-do-people-hate-smart-women

MacMillan Dictionary. "Career Woman." https://www.macmillandictionary.com/us/dictionary/american/career-woman

Organ, M. 2017. "Pantene Philippines 'Labels Against Women' Case Study." https://causemarketing.com/case-study/pantene-philippines-labels-women-case-study

Park, A. 2017. "Allure the Internet is Loving this New Word for When a Man Repeats your Idea and Gets Credit." https://www.allure.com/story/hepeat-twitter-reactions

RBG movie. n.d. https://www.rbgmovie.com

Reynolds, M. 2011. "Huffington Post Three Ways Women Can Better Manage their Careers," https://www.huffingtonpost.com/marcia-reynolds/women-career-advice_b_868531.html

Righthand, J. 2010. "How Annie Oakley the Princess of West Preserved Her Ladylike Reputation," *Smithsonian.Com*. https://www.smithsonianmag.com/history/how-annie-oakley-princess-of-the-west-preserved-her-ladylike-reputation-55701906

Soodalter, R. 2017. "HistoryNet Annie Oakley vs. Hearst's Worst." http://www.historynet.com/annie-oakley-vs-hearsts-worst.htm

Tempest, N., and K. L. McGinn. 2010. "Heidi Rozen Leadership & Managing People Case Study," *Harvard Business Review*. https://hbr.org/product/heidi-roizen/800228-PDF-ENG

The Annie Oakley Center Foundation, Inc. "Frequently asked questions about Annie Oakley," https://www.annieoakleycenterfoundation.com/faq6.html

Chapter 4

Colantuono, S. 2013. "Ted Talks the Career Advice You Probably Didn't Get." https://www.youtube.com/watch?v=JFQLvbVJVMg&t=19s

De Pater, I., A. E. M. Van Vianen, and M. N. Bechtoldt. 2010. "Tilburg University Gender Differences in Job Challenge: A Matter of Task Allocation." https://www.tilburguniversity.edu/upload/e49c2b37-b321-431b-8bca-a93ded3dd85d_onderzoek%20-%20gender%20differences%20in%20job%20challange.pdf

Desilver, D. 2018. "Women Scarce at Top of U.S. Business—and in the Jobs that Lead There," *Pew Research Center*. http://www.pewresearch.org/fact-tank/2018/04/30/women-scarce-at-top-of-u-s-business-and-in-the-jobs-that-lead-there

Gallo A. 2015. "Setting the Record Straight on Switching Jobs," *Harvard Business Review*. https://hbr.org/2015/07/setting-the-record-straight-on-switching-jobs

Hagemann, B. 2014. "I Wish I Could But I Can't." https://www.human-talentnetwork.com/wish-cant-thoughts-empowerment-of-women/6296/#content-anchor

Hosie, R. 2017. "Women are Better Leaders than Men Study of 3,000 Managers Concludes." https://www.independent.co.uk/life-style/women-better-leaders-men-study-a7658781.html

Immen, W. 2010. "Setting Career Goals the Gender Factor." https://www.theglobeandmail.com/report-on-business/careers/career-advice/setting-career-goals-the-gender-factor/article567903

Park, A. 2017. "Researchers Find Women Make Better Surgeons than Men." http://time.com/4975232/women-surgeon-surgery

Wood, G. 2000. "Sex Differences in Explanations for Career Progress," *Emerald Insight*. https://www.emeraldinsight.com/doi/abs/10.1108/09649420110392136?fullSc=1&journalCode=wimr

Chapter 5

Arts, B., A. Goodall and A. Oswald. 2018. "Research Women Ask for Raises as Often as Men, but are Less Likely to Get Them," *Harvard Business Review*. https://hbr.org/2018/06/research-women-ask-for-raises-as-often-as-men-but-are-less-likely-to-get-them

Bort, J. 2018. "How Uber's Top Lawyer Negotiated a Spectacular Severance Deal on Her Way Out the Door by Asking Travis Kalanick for about $100 million," *Business Insider*. http://www.businessinsider.com/uber-lawyer-salle-yoo-asked-for-100-million-and-got-a-great-severance-2018-3

Estrin, S., U. Stephan, and S. Vujic. 2014. "Do Women Earn Less Even as Social Entrepreneurs?" *Center for Economic Performance*. http://cep.lse.ac.uk/pubs/download/dp1313.pdf

Gorman, M. 2018. "Millennial Women are Poised to Be the Most Financially Independent Women in History," *Forbes Magazine*. https://www.forbes.com/sites/megangorman/2018/09/09/millennial-women-are-poised-to-be-the-most-financially-independent-women-in-history

Graf, N., A. Brown, and E. Patten. 2018. "The Narrowing, but Persistent, Gender Gap in Pay," *Pew Research Center*. http://www.pewresearch .org/fact-tank/2018/04/09/gender-pay-gap-facts

Kanze, D., L. Huang, M. Conley, E. T. Higgins. 2017. "Male and Female Entrepreneurs Asked Different Questions by VCs—and it Affects How Much Funding They Get." https://hbr.org/2017/06/male-and-female-entrepreneurs-get-asked-different-questions-by-vcs-and-it-affects-how-much-funding-they-get

McGinn, K., M. Ruiz, and E. Lingo. 2018. "Learning from Mum: Cross-National Evidence Linking Maternal Employment and Adult Children's Outcomes." http://journals.sagepub.com/doi/abs/10.1177/0950017018760167

Murphy, H. 2018. "Picture a Leader. Is She a Woman?" https://mobile .nytimes.com/2018/03/16/health/women-leadership-workplace.html

Selingo, J. 2017. "Six Myths about Choosing a College Major." https:// www.nytimes.com/2017/11/03/education/edlife/choosing-a-college-major.html

Stevenson, J. E., and E. Orr. 2017. "We Interviewed 57 Female CEOs to Find Out How More Women Can Get to the Top." https://hbr .org/2017/11/we-interviewed-57-female-ceos-to-find-out-how-more-women-can-get-to-the-top

Taylor, M. 2016. "Why Your Personality Is Getting in the Way of a Promotion." https://www.theguardian.com/sustainable-business/2016/oct/15/women-workplace-promotions-raises-mckinsey-leanin-study

Chapter 6

Alberty, E., and C. Ingraham. 2018. "The Washington Post and the Salt Lake Tribune Utah is the Second Most Sexist State Researchers Say–and Women's Internalized Sexism Appears to Play a Unique Role Here," https://www.sltrib.com/news/2018/08/21/researchers-identify-most

Cleur, C. 2018. "Overcoming Bias to Close the Gender Gap." https:// focus.kornferry.com/talent-acquisition/overcoming-bias-to-close-the-gender-gap-2

Cooper, S. 2018. *How to Be Successful without Hurting Men's Feelings: Non-threatening Leadership Strategies for Women Paperback.* Kansas, MO: Andrews McMeel Publishing.

Kahneman, D. 2011. *Thinking Fast and Slow.* New York, NY: Farrar, Straus and Giroux.

King, E., and K. Jones. 2016. "Why Subtle Bias is So Often Worse than Blatant Discrimination," *Harvard Business Review.* https://hbr.org/2016/07/why-subtle-bias-is-so-often-worse-than-blatant-discrimination

McCann, A. 2018. "The Best and Worst States for Women's Equality," *Wallet Hub.* https://wallethub.com/edu/best-and-worst-states-for-women-equality/5835

Rimbey, B., and S. Ghag. 2016. "How Women Can Overcome Bias at Work." https://www.gsb.stanford.edu/insights/how-women-can-overcome-bias-work

Chapter 7

Ernst & Young. 2015. "Study Work-Life Challenges across Generations: Millennials and Parents Hit Hardest." https://www.ey.com/us/en/about-us/our-people-and-culture/ey-work-life-challenges-across-generations-global-study

Friedersdorf, C. 2014. "Why PepsiCo CEO Indra K. Nooyi Can't Have It All." https://www.theatlantic.com/business/archive/2014/07/why-pepsico-ceo-indra-k-nooyi-cant-have-it-all/373750

Grice, M. M., P. M. McGovern, B. H. Alexander, L. Ukestad, and W. Hellerstedt. 2011. "Balancing Work and Family After Childbirth: A Longitudinal Analysis," *Women's Health Issues* 21, no. 1, pp. 19–27. www.whijournal.com/article/S1049-3867(10)00117-9/fulltext

Groysberg, B., and R. Abrahams. 2014. "Manage Your Work, Manage Your Life," *Harvard Business Review.* https://hbr.org/2014/03/manage-your-work-manage-your-life

Henion, A. 2013. "Single Employees Want Work-Life Balance, Too," *Michigan State University.* www.futurity.org/single-employees-want-work-life-balance-too

Keeney, J., E. M. Boyd, R. Sinha, A. F. Westring, and A. Ryan. 2013. "From 'Work-Family' to 'Work-Life': Broadening Our Conceptualization

and Measurement." www.sciencedirect.com/science/article/abs/pii/
S0001879113000274

Lekushoff, A. 2013. "HuffPost Eight Steps to a Better Work-Life Balance for Women." https://www.huffingtonpost.ca/andrea-lekushoff/balance-family-and-career_b_4104575.html

Moyes, N. 2013. "LinkedIn What Women Want @ Work." https://blog.linkedin.com/2013/02/28/linkedin-what-women-want-study

Murdoch, C. 2012. "Work-Life Balance Isn't Just for Moms Anymore: Single Ladies Want It Too." https://jezebel.com/5912572/work-life-balance-isnt-just-for-moms-anymore-all-the-single-ladies-want-it-too

National Alliance for Caregiving in Collaboration with AARP. 2009. "Caregiving in the U.S. Executive Summary." www.caregiving.org/pdf/research/CaregivingUSAllAgesExecSum.pdf

Olver, C. 2011. "Changes in Time Allocation among American Families," *Journalist's Resource UCLA Study*, https://journalistsresource.org/studies/society/gender-society/family-time-allocation-american-families

Pew Research Center. 2013. "Modern Parenthood: Roles of Moms and Dads Converge as they Balance Work and Family." http://www.pewsocialtrends.org/2013/03/14/modern-parenthood-roles-of-moms-and-dads-converge-as-they-balance-work-and-family

Slaughter, A. July/August, 2012. "The Atlantic Why Women Still Can't Have It All." www.theatlantic.com/magazine/archive/2012/07/why-women-still-cant-have-it-all/309020

Society for Human Resources Management. 2015. "SHRM Research: Flexible Work Arrangements." https://www.shrm.org/hr-today/trends-and-forecasting/special-reports-and-expert-views/Documents/Flexible%20Work%20Arrangements.pdf

Sundaresan, S. 2014. "Work-Life Balance—Implications for Working Women." www.researchgate.net/publication/272845610_WORK-LIFE_BALANCE_-_IMPLICATIONS_FOR_WORKING_WOMEN

Van Zandt, E. 2018. "Washington Business Journal Viewpoint: No Kids? You Deserve Work-Life Balance, Too." www.bizjournals.com/washington/news/2018/06/21/viewpoint-no-kids-you-deserve-work-life-balance.html

Chapter 8

Cain, A. 2017. "Business Insider 16 Signs that Your Coworker is Undermining You." https://www.businessinsider.com/signs-you-are-being-undermined-at-work-2017-6

Doityourself.com. "How to Make Homemade Bee Repellent." https://www.doityourself.com/stry/how-to-make-homemade-bee-repellent

Dolan, C., and F. Oliver. 2009. "How to Stop the 'Mean Girls' in the Workplace." *Harvard Business Review*, https://hbr.org/2009/10/how-to-stop-mean-girls-in-the

FlourishAnyway. 2018. "Office Mean Girl: Memories of a Workplace Bully." https://toughnickel.com/business/Office-Mean-Girl-Memories-of-a-Workplace-Bully

Gabriel, A. S., M. M. Butts, Z. Yuan, R. L. Rosen, and M. T. Sliter. 2018. "Further Understanding Incivility in the Workplace: The Effects of Gender, Agency, and Communion." *Journal of Applied Psychology* 103, no. 4, pp. 362–382. http://psycnet.apa.org/doiLanding?doi=10.1037%2Fapl0000289

Harvey, C. 2018. "When Queen Bees Attack Women Stop Advancing: Recognizing and Addressing Female Bullying in the Workplace." https://www.emeraldinsight.com/doi/full/10.1108/DLO-04-2018-0048

Harvey, C. 2018. "'Queen Bees' Hinder Women in the Workplace." https://economia.icaew.com/opinion/april-2018/queen-bees-hinder-women-in-the-workplace

Huang, G. "How to Deal with Mean Girls and Catty Colleagues at Work," *FairyGodBoss Blog*. https://fairygodboss.com/articles/mean-girls-at-work

Khazan, O. 2017. "Why Do Women Bully Each Other at Work? Research Suggests that Conditions in the Workplace Might Be to Blame," https://www.theatlantic.com/magazine/archive/2017/09/the-queen-bee-in-the-corner-office/534213

O'Reilly, N. Dr. n.d. "Why Are Women So Mean to Other Women?" https://www.drnancyoreilly.com/why-are-women-so-mean-to-other-women/

Sandberg, S., and A. Grant. 2016. "Sheryl Sandberg on the Myth of the Catty Woman," *New York Times*. https://www.nytimes.com/2016/06/23/opinion/sunday/sheryl-sandberg-on-the-myth-of-the-catty-woman.html

Schmitz, A. 2018. "University of Arizona Is 'Queen Bee' Syndrome Getting Worse?" https://www.eurekalert.org/pub_releases/2018-03/uoa-iaw030118.php

Settembre, J. 2018. "What to do if you Work for a Queen Bee." https://www.marketwatch.com/story/what-to-do-if-you-work-for-a-queen-bee-2018-08-06

Sharkey, L. 2018. "Evolution or Sexism: Why are so Many Female Bosses 'Queen Bees'?" https://metro.co.uk/2018/05/24/evolution-or-sexism-why-are-so-many-female-bosses-queen-bees-7548191

Stringer, M. 2017. "Mean Girls Become Mean Women: How to Protect Yourself from Adult Regina Georges," https://metro.co.uk/2017/06/09/mean-girls-become-mean-women-how-to-protect-yourself-from-adult-regina-georges-6679929

Thrope, J. R. 2018. "What is 'Queen Bee Syndrome?' It Might Explain Why Some Women are Uncivil to Each Other at Work." https://www.bustle.com/p/what-is-queen-bee-syndrome-it-might-explain-why-some-women-are-uncivil-to-each-other-at-work-8402852

Whimn, J. 2018. "New York Post 'Queen Bees' are Holding Women Back in the Workplace," https://nypost.com/2018/08/27/queen-bees-are-holding-women-back-in-the-workplace

Chapter 9

AAUW. 2018. "Barrier and Bias: The Status of Women in Leadership." https://www.aauw.org/research/barriers-and-bias

Anderson, R. J., and W. A. Adams. 2016. "Sink or Swim: Setting First Time Leaders Up For Success." https://www.clomedia.com/2016/08/31/sink-or-swim-setting-first-time-leaders-up-for-success

Eagly, A. 2013. "Gender and Work: Challenging Conventional Wisdom," *Harvard Business School.* https://www.hbs.edu/faculty/conferences/2013-w50-research-symposium/Documents/eagly.pdf

Frankel, D. 2006. *The Devil Wears Prada* (Movie).

Horowitz, J. M., R. Igielnik, and K. Parker. 2018. "Women and Leadership 2018: Wide Gender and Party Gaps in views about the state of female leadership and the obstacles women face," *Pew Research Center.* http://www.pewsocialtrends.org/2018/09/20/women-and-leadership-2018

Keller, S., and M. Meany. 2018. "Successfully Transitioning to New Leadership Roles," *McKinsey & Company*. https://www.mckinsey .com/business-functions/organization/our-insights/successfully-transitioning-to-new-leadership-roles

Knowledge@Wharton, University of Pennsylvania. 2005. "The 'Masculine' and 'Feminine' Sides of Leadership and Culture: Perception vs. Reality." http://knowledge.wharton.upenn.edu/article/the-masculine-and-feminine-sides-of-leadership-and-culture-perception-vs-reality

Moral Ethics. 2013. "Ford Pinto Case." https://moralethics101.wordpress .com/2013/05/24/ford-pinto-case

Nink, M. 2018. "Who Makes a Better Boss, Him or Her?" *Gallup*, https://www.gallup.com/workplace/236234/makes-better-boss.aspx

Readers Read. 2018. "Interview with Lauren Weisberger about the Devil Wears Prada." https://www.writerswrite.com/books/interview-with-lauren-weisberger-about-the-devil-wears-prada-40120032

Science News. 2018. "University of Buffalo Men are Still More Likely to be Perceived as Effective Leaders: Despite Progress Gender Gap in Leadership Exists." https://www.sciencedaily.com/releases/2018/08/180809144524.htm

Sellers, P., and J. Shambora. 2009. "Behind the Fortune 500s First Female CEO Handoff." http://fortune.com/2009/05/21/behind-the-fortune-500s-first-female-ceo-handoff

The Myers Briggs Company. n.d. https://www.themyersbriggs.com

Zheng, W., O. Surgevil, and R. Kark. 2018. "Dancing on the Razor's Edge: How Top-Level Women Leaders Manage the Paradoxical Tensions between Agency and Communion." *Sex Roles* 79, no. 11–12, pp. 633–650. https://link.springer.com/article/10.1007%2Fs11199-018-0908-6

Chapter 10

Babcock, P. 2011. "Study Probes Bullying of HR Professionals." https://www.shrm.org/resourcesandtools/hr-topics/risk-management/pages/bullyinghrprofessionals.aspx

Clink, K. 2013. "Woman Suffrage Portrayed in Textbooks," Minnesota State University, Mankato. https://cornerstone.lib.mnsu.edu/cgi/viewcontent.cgi?article=1011&context=lib_services_fac_pubs

Kane, S. 2018. "Who is a Workplace Bully's Target? Defend Yourself against Workplace Bullies." https://www.thebalancecareers.com/who-is-a-workplace-bully-s-target-2164323

Leyshock, S., and R. Ablin. 2018. "When Employers Hear #MeToo: Top 10 Tips on How to Respond," *American Bar Association.* https://www.americanbar.org/groups/litigation/committees/woman-advocate/articles/2018/employers-10-tips-metoo/

Namie, G. 2017. "The 2017 Workplace Bullying Institute U.S. Workplace Bullying Survey," *Employer and Witness Reactions.* http://www.workplacebullying.org/multi/pdf/2017/E&W-Reactions.pdf

Samara, M., V. Burbidge, A. El Asam, M. Foody, P. Smith, and M. Hisham. 2017. "Bullying and Cyberbullying: Their Legal Status and Use in Psychological Assessment." *International Journal of Environmental Research and Public Health* 14, no. 12, pp. 1449. https://www.ncbi.nlm.nih.gov/pmc/articles/PMC5750868

Sutton, R. 2007. "Why I Wrote the No Asshole Rule," *Harvard Business Review.* https://hbr.org/2007/03/why-i-wrote-the-no-asshole-rule

U.S. Equal Employment Opportunity Commission. 2017. "FY 2017." https://www.eeoc.gov/eeoc/statistics/enforcement/sexual_harassment_new.cfm

Yaribeygi, H., Y. Panahi, H. Sahraei, T. Johnston, and A. Sahebkar. 2017. "The Impact of Stress on Body Function. A Review," U.S. National Library of Medicine. National Institutes of Health. https://www.ncbi.nlm.nih.gov/pmc/articles/PMC5579396

About the Author

Saundra Stroope is a consultant and coach. Her passion for development, drive for results, business acumen, and more than 20 years of human capital experience—in a variety of industries and award-winning global and Fortune 500 companies—allow her to bring creative ideas and practical talent solutions to the organizations she works with. She is the author of more than a dozen works on career, leadership, teams, and development of high-potential emerging leaders.

Saundra has experience in leadership development, succession planning, culture change, organization development, employee engagement, career development, team development, curriculum design, facilitation, human resources, and coaching individuals at all leadership levels. She has a long track record of leading and measuring the success of talent development initiatives.

Saundra holds a bachelor's degree in psychology and a master's degree in human resources management from Texas A&M University. She is certified in the use of many leadership development programs and coaching assessments. Her certifications and qualifications include: Myers-Briggs Type Indicator® (MBTI®) Step I™ and Step II™; Fundamental Interpersonal Relations Orientation™ (FIRO®); Strong Interest Inventory®; Thomas-Kilmann Conflict Mode Instrument (TKI®); CPI 260®; PDI Profiler, Lominger, and DecisionWise 360 Feedback Assessments; Certified Facilitator for Crucial Conversations, People Skills, InsideOut Coaching, DDI, AchieveGlobal, Career Systems International Love 'Em or Lose 'Em, Learning Point Leadership Boot Camp, and Catalyst Learning NCharge Nurse Leadership; DISC and Insights Profiles; Watson Glaser Critical Thinking and Thinking Styles Profiles by Pearson TalentLens; and Human Resources Certification Institute PHR, Professional in Human Resources, certification.

Index

Pantyhose are BS

—Anonymous survey respondent

OTHER TITLES IN THE HUMAN RESOURCE MANAGEMENT AND ORGANIZATIONAL BEHAVIOR COLLECTION

- *Leading the High-Performing Company: A Transformational Guide to Growing Your Business and Outperforming Your Competition* by Heidi Pozzo
- *How Successful Engineers Become Great Business Leaders* by Paul Rulkens
- *Creating a Successful Consulting Practice* by Gary W. Randazzo
- *Skilling India: Challenges and Opportunities* by S. Nayana Tara
- *Redefining Competency Based Education: Competence for Life* by Nina Morel
- *No Dumbing Down: A No-Nonsense Guide for CEOs on Organization Growth* by Karen D. Walker
- *From Behind the Desk to the Front of the Stage: How to Enhance Your Presentation Skills* by David Worsfold
- *The New World of Human Resources and Employment: How Artificial Intelligence and Process Redesign is Driving Dramatic Change* by Tony Miller
- *Virtual Vic: A Management Fable* by Laurence M. Rose
- *Our Glassrooms: Perceptiveness and Its Implications for Transformational Leadership* by Dhruva Trivedy
- *Leadership Insights: 11 Typical Mistakes Young Leaders Make and Tips to Avoid Them* by Matt L. Beadle
- *Temperatism, Volume II: Doing Good Through Business With a Social Conscience* by Carrie Foster
- *The Generation Myth: How to Improve Intergenerational Relationships in the Workplace* by Michael J. Urick
- *What Millennials Really Want From Work and Life* by Yuri Kruman
- *Practicing Leadership* by Alan S. Gutterman
- *Women Leaders: The Power of Working Abroad* by Sapna Welsh and Caroline Kersten

Announcing the Business Expert Press Digital Library

Concise e-books business students need for classroom and research

This book can also be purchased in an e-book collection by your library as

- *a one-time purchase,*
- *that is owned forever,*
- *allows for simultaneous readers,*
- *has no restrictions on printing, and*
- *can be downloaded as PDFs from within the library community.*

Our digital library collections are a great solution to beat the rising cost of textbooks. E-books can be loaded into their course management systems or onto students' e-book readers.
The **Business Expert Press** digital libraries are very affordable, with no obligation to buy in future years. For more information, please visit **www.businessexpertpress.com/librarians**. To set up a trial in the United States, please email **sales@businessexpertpress.com**.